Paper Piecing
Potpourri

Fun-Filled Projects for Every Quilter

From the Editors and Contributors
of *Quilter's Newsletter Magazine*
and *Quiltmaker Magazine*

C&T PUBLISHING

© 2003 Primedia Special Interest Publications
Editor-in-Chief: Darra Williamson
Editor: Diane Kennedy-Jackson
Proofreaders: Marsha Littleton, Susan Nelsen
Cover Designer: Kristen Yenche
Book Designer: Rohani Design
Design Director: Diane Pedersen
Original Illustrations: *Quilter's Newsletter Magazine* and *Quiltmaker* staff
Additional Illustrations: Kirstie L. McCormick
Production Assistant: Kristy A. Konitzer
Photography: Mellisa Karlin Mahony
Front Cover: *Folk Art Compass* by Chris Taricani
Back Cover: *Wagon Wheels* by Dixie Haywood and *Full Circle* by Tone Haugen-Cogburn

Library of Congress Cataloging-in-Publication Data

Paper piecing potpourri : fun-filled projects for every quilter / "From the Editors and Contributors of Quilter's Newsletter Magazine and Quiltmaker." editor, Diane Kennedy-Jackson.
    p. cm.
  ISBN 1-57120-188-2
  1. Quilting–Patterns. 2. Patchwork–Patterns. I. Kennedy-Jackson, Diane, 1963- II. Quilter's newsletter magazine. III. Quiltmaker.
  TT835 .P3515 2002
  746.46'041–dc21

                    2002011973

Published by C&T Publishing, Inc.
P.O. Box 1456
Lafayette, California 94549

Printed in China
10 9 8 7 6 5 4 3 2 1

Introduction

If you love quilts and quiltmaking, then *Paper Piecing Potpourri* is certain to delight your senses. Including seventeen quilts—from charming to breathtaking, from classic to contemporary—this compilation features designs that are among the best of the best from *Quiltmaker* magazine and *Quilter's Newsletter Magazine*.

Included in the pages ahead is a variety of quilt designs. Those whose tastes run to contemporary will find *Nancy's Garden* appealing. The designers of this quilt captured the look of stained glass in an oh-so-modern setting. For those who prefer patterns that display the rich history of quiltmaking, *Wagon Wheels* is sure to catch your eye. Adapted from a pattern that first appeared in the *Kansas City Star* in 1934, this design features traditional shapes adapted for paper-foundation piecing, which was unheard of at the time the original pattern appeared. Those in search of seasonal-decorating patterns will enjoy *Christmas Cardinals* and *Sparkling Candles*. The former features this striking winter bird in all its colorful splendor, while the latter was inspired by the Menorah and the traditional Jewish holiday of Hanukkah. *Shooting Stars* is bound to get the attention of those touched by a patriotic spirit, and *Drake Lake* will be ideal for that special man who is fond of the outdoors. Two of the designs, *Basket Bouquets* and *Promises*, feature extensive appliqué. Yet another, *Busting Out*, marks the journey of a breast-cancer survivor. What do they all have in common? Each holds a bit of history. Each has a story all its own.

Why not start your own bit of history, your own story, with some of the many designs included in *Paper Piecing Potpourri*? The editors of C&T Publishing believe you'll find a host of projects to inspire you, whether you're just getting started quilting or you have been creating family heirlooms for as long as you can remember.

Contents

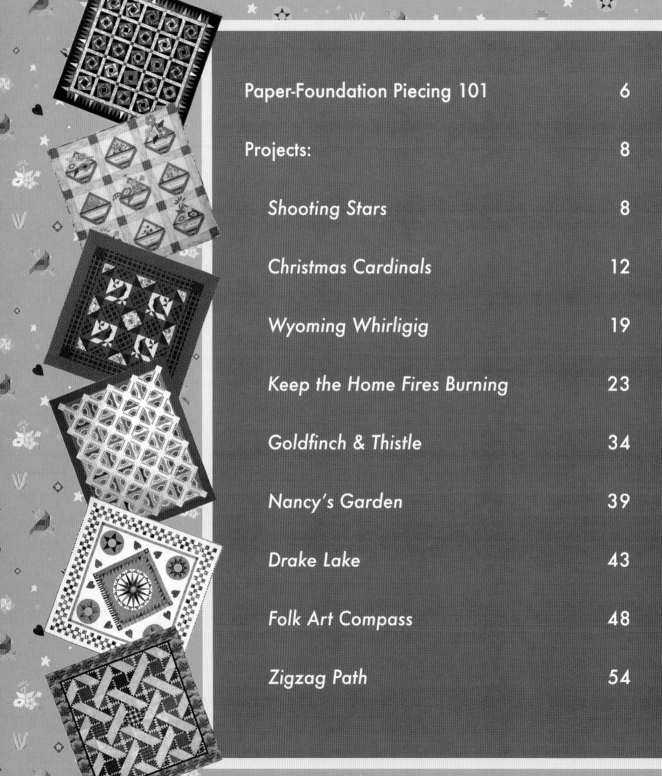

Paper-Foundation Piecing 101

by Barbara Fiedler

Foundation piecing is an accurate technique for sewing blocks that are difficult to piece. A little practice and knowing a few "do's and don'ts" will make you successful with this popular technique.

To help you understand this piecing method, study this foundation-pieced block and the illustrations of common foundation-piecing mistakes. For instruction, the correct stitching is shown in black and incorrect sewing is marked in red. It doesn't take long to master this technique; you'll be passing PFP 101 in one easy lesson.

1. **Trace or photocopy the complete foundation pattern, including all the numbers and lines.** Without the block seam lines or cutting lines, you will not know where to sew or where to trim the block to its correct size.

2. **Cut out the paper foundation beyond the outer line.** The extra dimension is a good visual measure of size for those patches that lie along the block perimeter. If your patches extend beyond the foundation, you know they will be large enough.

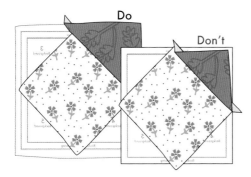

3. **Always set your stitch length to a short setting, 18–20 stitches to the inch.** ┅┅┅┅┅┅ Longer stitches won't perforate the paper close enough so it will be harder to tear away the foundation and easier for the stitches to pull loose.

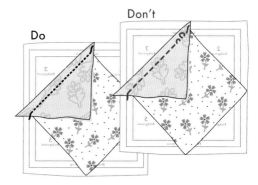

4. **Check patch placement before you sew it to the foundation.** If not, you could sew a patch with a seam allowance that is too narrow or miss sewing the patch to the foundation.

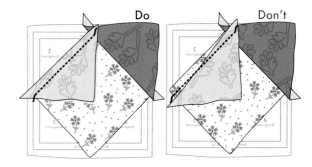

5. **Stitch on the printed side of the foundation to easily follow the sewing line and sew exactly on the printed seam line.** Sewing off the line will change the pattern or design.

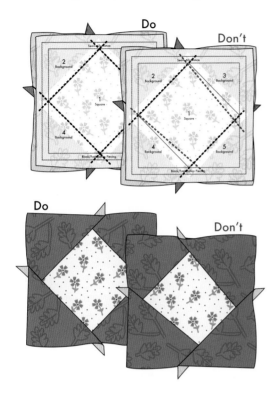

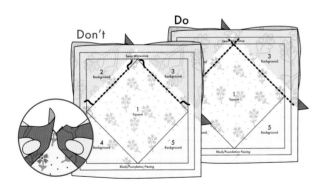

6. **For every seam line, begin stitching ¼" before the seam line and continue ¼" beyond.** If the stitching does not cross over the previous seam line, as consecutive patches are added a gap will exist in the patchwork. Backstitching does not take the place of cross seaming.

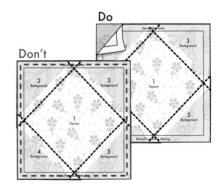

7. **After each patch addition, trim the seam allowances to ¼".** Narrower seam allowances

can pull away from the stitching and leave a hole in the block.

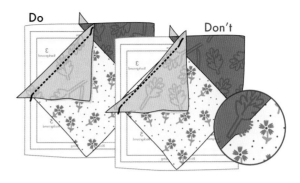

8. **After a patch is added, open the patch from the fabric side and press the seam flat.** Otherwise, you will have a tuck in the fabric and patches will not be the correct size.

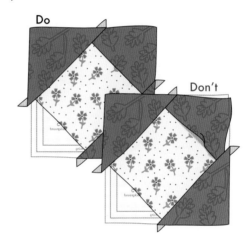

9. **Trim the foundation precisely on the outside line after it is pieced.** Careless cutting will give an inaccurate block size.

10. **Leave the outer foundation lines unsewn.** If you stitch the foundation perimeter, removing the paper will be difficult.

Note: Photocopying may cause distortion. Compare pattern copies to original for accuracy.

Shooting Stars

by Mickie Swall

BEGINNER ◆

To celebrate the July birthday of *Quiltmaker* magazine senior editor Jan Magee, Mickie Swall created a red, white, and blue quilt, with a bit of cheddar gold added to the mix, that was quick and easy to make. Magee noted that because she can't decide which she loves more—piecing or appliqué—she wanted the quilt to have both. This design also provided an opportunity to experiment with blocks that weren't square. *Shooting Stars* met all of the requirements.

Designed and made by Mickie Swall.

MATERIALS AND CUTTING

Block Sizes:		7½" x 7½", 4" x 7½"
Quilt Size:		63" x 79"

Requirements are based on 42" fabric width.

Borders are the exact length required plus seam allowances.

Read all instructions before cutting. Cut foundation-piecing patches ¾" larger than pattern.

Materials	Yards	Cutting
Red Print	5	
foundation-piecing		#1, 3, 5, 7, 8 patches
Tan Solid	2⅓	
foundation-piecing		#2, 4, 6 patches
Gold Solid	1⅞	
inner borders (sides)		2 at 2½" x 60½"
inner borders (top/bottom)		2 at 2½" x 48½"
stars		48 A, 44 B, 44 Br patches
Navy Print	2⅛	44 X blocks 5" x 8½"; 4 Z blocks 8½" x 8½"
Navy/Tan Stripe	⅝	
binding		8 strips 2¼" x 42"
Backing	4⅞	2 panels 34" x 83"
Batting		67" x 83"

Tip Deep red and blue with tan and cheddar gold give the assembled quilt the antique look of patriotic memorabilia. For a more-contemporary look, substitute bright red, royal blue, white, and yellow.

Getting Started

Wash and press fabrics. Cut the stars and other pieces as listed in the materials and cutting box. Refer to page 92 for Quilting Basics.

Making the Blocks

1. Trace or photocopy seventy-two block Y and twenty-eight reverse block Y for block Yr.

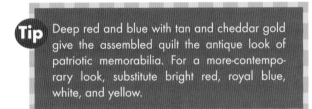

Block Y
Make 72

Block Yr
Make 28

2. Foundation-piece the fabric units in numerical order.

3. Prepare A, B, and Br stars for appliqué using your favorite method.

4. Appliqué the A, B, and Br stars to block X. Appliqué the A star to block Z.

Block X
Make 44

Block Z
Make 4

5. Measuring out from the center, trim X blocks to 4½" x 8" and Z blocks to 8" x 8".

Assembling the Quilt Top

1. Join the X and Y blocks, referring to row assembly, to make row 1.
2. Join upside-down X and Y blocks, referring to row assembly, to make row 2.

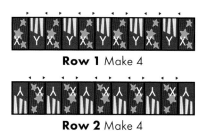

Row 1 Make 4

Row 2 Make 4
Row Assembly

3. Press the seam allowances as indicated in row assembly.
4. Join the rows, beginning with row 1 and alternating row types.
5. Sew the inner borders to the sides of the quilt and trim. Sew the inner borders to the top and bottom and trim. Press the seam allowances toward the borders.
6. Join the Y and Yr blocks to make side pieced borders, referring to border assembly.

Side Pieced Border Make 2

7. Join the Y, Yr, and Z blocks to make the top and bottom pieced borders, referring to border assembly. Press the seam allowances as indicated in border assembly.

Top/Bottom Pieced Border Make 2

8. Sew the pieced side borders to the sides of the quilt. Press the seam allowances toward the inner border. Sew the pieced top and bottom borders to the top and bottom. Press the seam allowances toward the inner border.
9. Remove the paper.

Quilting and Finishing

1. Layer and baste the quilt backing, batting, and top.
2. To quilt without marking the fabric, make quilting templates from adhesive shelf-liner paper. Trace B and Br several times and A at least four times on adhesive paper. Cut out the shapes. Working one vertical row of blocks at a time, place adhesive-paper A stars on the Y blocks. Outline quilt the stars and quilt the Y blocks in-the-ditch, traveling down the left side of the stars and back up on the right in a continuous line. Refer to quilting placement. Move the paper A stars to the next vertical row of blocks and repeat until the quilting in the center of the quilt is complete. Quilt the border patches in-the-ditch in a continuous line around the perimeter of the quilt. Place adhesive-paper stars randomly around the quilt edges, making sure to place two in each Z block. Quilt around the stars in the border.

Quilting Placement

3. Trim quilt backing and batting even with the quilt top.
4. Join 2¼"-wide strips diagonally to make the binding. Bind the quilt.

Add 3/16" turn-under allowances to all appliqué stars.

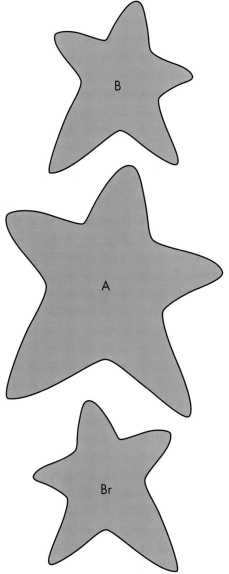

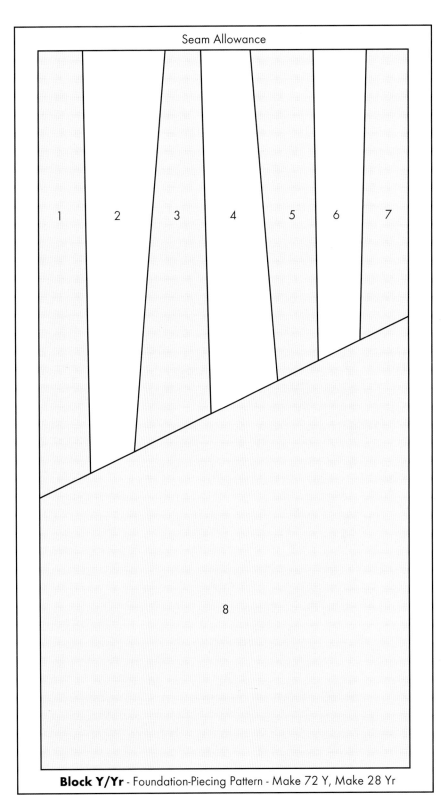

Seam Allowance

1 2 3 4 5 6 7

8

Block Y/Yr - Foundation-Piecing Pattern - Make 72 Y, Make 28 Yr

Christmas Cardinals

BEGINNER ◆

by Becky Anderson

Perfect for the winter holidays, *Christmas Cardinals* will look great year-round too! The technique of paper-foundation piecing will help busy quilters make these colorful, feathered friends in a flash.

Short on time? A single cardinal block surrounded by a plaid border will lend a hint of the holidays wherever it's displayed.

Designed by Becky Anderson. Sewn by Nancy Fisher and Jan Magee.

MATERIALS AND CUTTING

Block Size: 7½" x 7½"

Quilt Size: 39" x 39"

Requirements are based on 42" fabric width.

Borders are the exact length required plus seam allowances.

Read all instructions before cutting. Cut foundation-piecing patches ¾" larger than pattern.

Materials	Yards	Cutting
Cream Print	5/8	
foundation-piecing		2 each #2, 4, 5, 7, 9, 14, 15, 17, 18, 22, 24, 26, 28 patches for W blocks and for Y blocks
Cream/Red Print	3/8	
foundation-piecing		#1 patch for Z block; 4 #1 patches for border unit 1; 4 #1 patches for border unit 3
Dark Green Print	5/8	
border corner squares		4 at 4" x 4"
foundation-piecing		2 each #1, 25 patches for W blocks and for Y blocks; 1 each #2, 3, 4, 5 patches for Z block; 4 #2 patches for border unit 1; 4 each #2, 3 patches for border unit 3
Medium Green Print	1/4	
foundation-piecing		2 each #6, 8, 16, 25 patches for W blocks and for Y blocks
Red Print #1	1 3/8	
inner borders (sides)		2 at 1½" x 30½"
inner borders (top/bottom)		2 at 1½" x 32½"
binding		5 strips 2¼" x 42"
foundation-piecing		4 each #2, 3, 4, 5 patches for X blocks; 8 each #2, 3 patches for border unit 2
Red Print #2	3/8	
foundation-piecing		2 each #3, 10, 11, 13, 21 patches for W blocks and for Y blocks
Dark Red Print	1/4	
foundation-piecing		2 each #12, 19 patches for W blocks and for Y blocks
Red/Green Plaid*	1	
outer borders (sides)		2 at 4" x 32½"
outer borders (top/bottom)		2 at 4" x 32½"
foundation-piecing		4 #1 patches for X blocks; 8 #1 patches for border unit 2
Gold Solid Scraps		
foundation-piecing		2 #27 patches for W blocks and for Y blocks
Black Solid Scraps		
foundation-piecing		2 #20 patches for W blocks and for Y blocks
Backing	2 ½	
backing		2 panels 22" x 43"
sleeve		9" x 39"
Batting		43" x 43"

* Before cutting borders and patches from plaid fabric, refer to Matching Plaids on page 15. Plaid is shown as solid green in the illustration.

Getting Started

Wash and press fabrics. Cut the patches and other pieces as listed in the materials and cutting box. Refer to page 92 for Quilting Basics.

Making the Blocks

1. Trace or photocopy two W blocks, two Y blocks, a total of five X or Z blocks (the block pattern is the same; the coloration makes the blocks different), four border unit 1, and a total of twelve border units 2 and 3 (again, the block pattern is the same; the coloration makes the blocks different).

2. For each W block, foundation-piece the patches by section in numerical order. Join the sections to make a block.

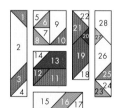

Block W Piecing
Make 2

3. For each Y block, foundation-piece the patches by section in numerical order. Join the sections to make a block.

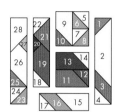

Block Y Piecing
Make 2

4. For each X or Z block, foundation-piece the patches in numerical order.

Block X Piecing   **Block Z Piecing**
Make 4   Make 1

5. Foundation-piece the border units, sewing the patches in numerical order and referring to the appropriate border unit piecing for color placement.

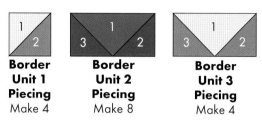

Border Unit 1 Piecing
Make 4

Border Unit 2 Piecing
Make 8

Border Unit 3 Piecing
Make 4

6. Trim all dark seam allowances to be narrower than light seam allowances.

Assembling the Quilt Top

1. Join the W, X, Y, and Z blocks in three horizontal rows of three blocks each, referring to the quilt assembly for block placement.

2. Join the rows.

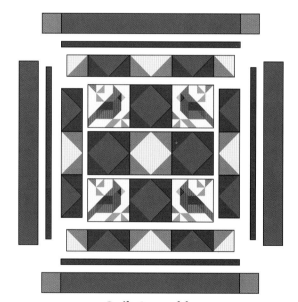

Quilt Assembly

3. Join the border units, referring to the quilt assembly for unit placement.

4. Sew the assembled border units to the sides, top, and bottom of the quilt.

5. Sew the inner borders to the sides of the quilt. Sew the inner borders to the top and bottom. Press the seam allowances toward the borders.

6. Sew the outer borders to the sides of the quilt. Sew border-corner squares to the ends of remaining outer borders and sew assembled outer borders to the top and bottom. Press the seam allowances toward the inner borders.

7. Remove the paper.

Quilting and Finishing

1. Layer and baste the quilt backing, batting, and top.

2. Quilt in-the-ditch around the patches. For plaid patches and borders, choose some lines of the plaid and quilt along them. Quilt in-the-ditch next to the borders and the border-corner squares.

3. Trim quilt backing and batting even with the quilt top.

4. Join 2¼"-wide strips diagonally to make the binding. Bind the quilt.

5. Sew a sleeve to the backing for display purposes.

Matching Plaids

In *Christmas Cardinals,* the placement of the plaid fabric is the same from patch to patch and from border strip to border strip. If the plaid patches and borders are cut randomly, the irregularity will attract unwanted attention. By using the fabric-cutting technique for matching plaids, the cardinals remain the focus of the quilt. For a perfect match like this, each border strip and each plaid block patch must be cut from exactly the same part of the fabric design. Even though the blocks and units are made with

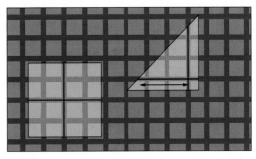

paper-foundation piecing, which does not require patches cut to exact shapes, those wishing to match plaids will want to make templates for the center square from the X block and the large triangle from border unit 2. Make the templates from see-through template plastic, making sure to add seam allowances.

For the square, mark the center lines as shown. Place the template on the right side of the plaid fabric, centering the template over a portion of the plaid. Mark placement lines on the template with a permanent pen. Cut out a square. Repeat to cut out identical squares for each X block. When piecing, center this square over the paper foundation and pin it so it will not shift.

For the large triangle used in border unit 2, first determine the desired positioning of the plaid on the patch. Place template on the plaid and choose a symmetrical position. Mark the lines on the template. Cut out large triangles for each border unit 2. When piecing, pin the patch over the paper foundation and pin it so it will not shift.

To achieve symmetry within the border strips, determine the portion of the plaid that will fall at the center point of a border strip. Measure each half of the border strip out from this center point. Cut all four borders in the same manner.

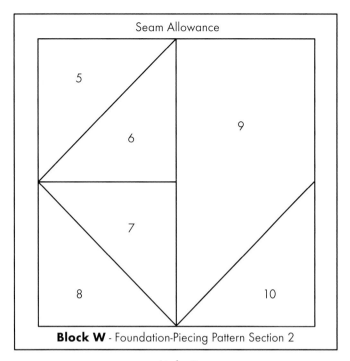

Seam Allowance

Block W - Foundation-Piecing Pattern Section 2

Make 2
Reverse for block Y

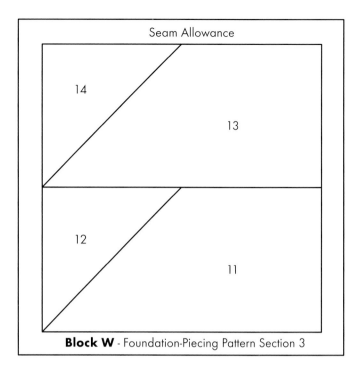

Seam Allowance

Block W - Foundation-Piecing Pattern Section 3

Make 2
Reverse for block Y

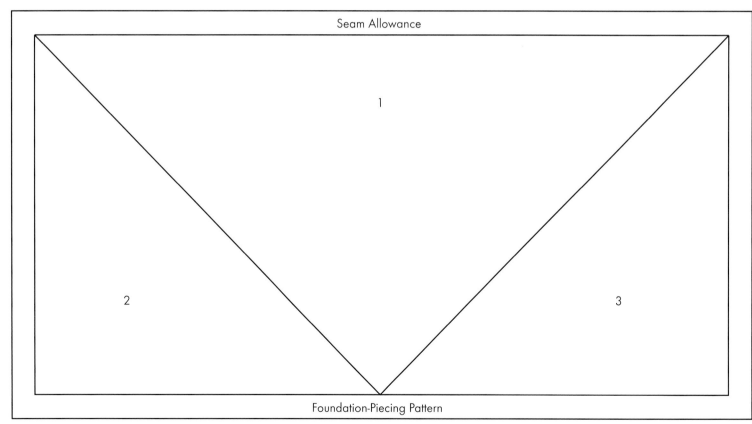

Seam Allowance

Foundation-Piecing Pattern

Border Unit 2 - Make 8, **Border Unit 3 -** Make 4
Patterns are the reverse of the finished block.

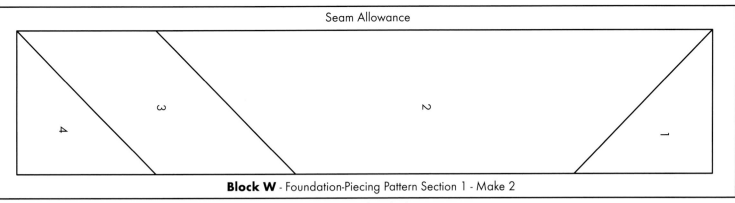

Seam Allowance

Block W - Foundation-Piecing Pattern Section 1 - Make 2

Reverse for Block Y

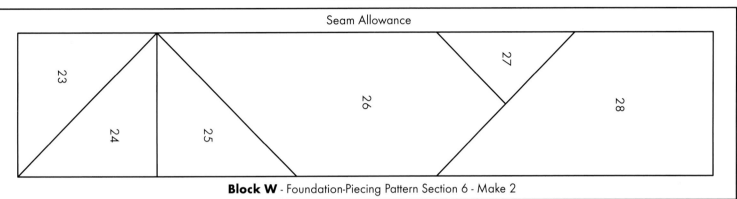

Seam Allowance

Block W - Foundation-Piecing Pattern Section 6 - Make 2

Reverse for Block Y

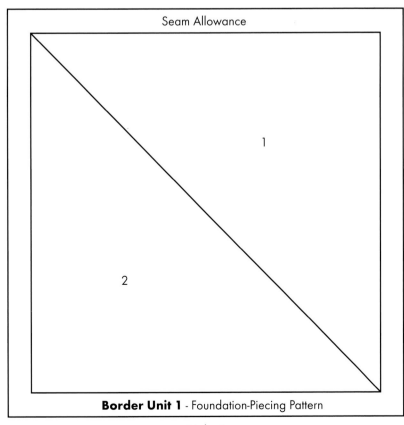

Seam Allowance

Border Unit 1 - Foundation-Piecing Pattern

Make 4

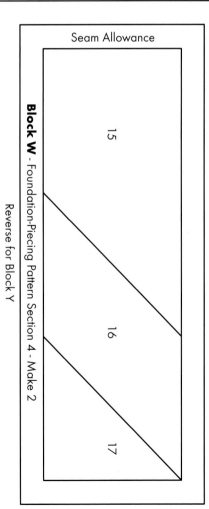

Seam Allowance

Block W - Foundation-Piecing Pattern Section 4 - Make 2

Reverse for Block Y

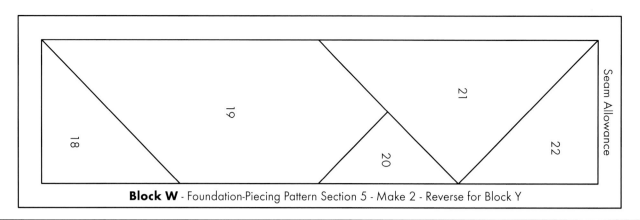

Block W - Foundation-Piecing Pattern Section 5 - Make 2 - Reverse for Block Y

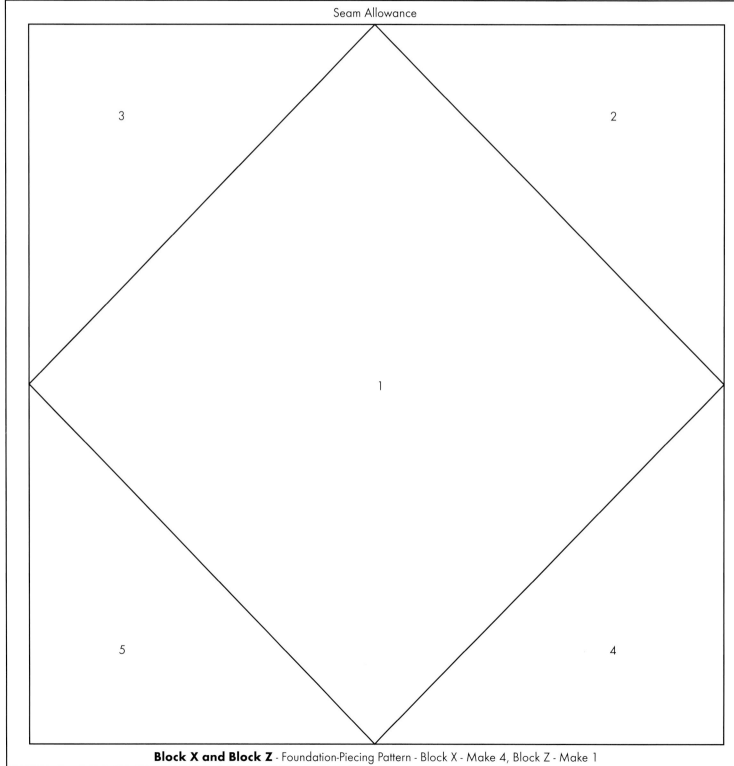

Block X and Block Z - Foundation-Piecing Pattern - Block X - Make 4, Block Z - Make 1

Wyoming Whirligig

BEGINNER ◆

This pattern was first published in *The Kansas City Star* in 1936 as *Whirling Hexagon* and again in 1943 as *Texas Trellis*. The name given to this quilt honors its makers, the women in the Davenport family of Laramie, Wyoming. The quilt is from the collection of Teri Coffman.

Block Size: 5" x 5¾"

Quilt Sizes: Double Comforter (shown), [Queen Coverlet]   83⅜" x 90" [92" x 110"]

Requirements are based on 42" fabric width.

Read all instructions before cutting. Cut foundation-piecing patches ¾" larger than pattern.

Materials	Yards	Cutting	Materials	Yards	Cutting
Double Comforter			**Queen Coverlet**		
Assorted Print Scraps	9½		Assorted Print Scraps	13	
each block		4" x 10"	each block		4" x 10"
Yellow Solid	5⅝	#2, 4, 6, background	Yellow Solid	6	#2, 4, 6, background
		patches			patches
bias binding		1¼" x 14 yards	bias binding		1¼" x 17¼ yards
Backing	7½	3 panels 32" x 88"	Backing	8⅛	3 panels 39" x 96"
Batting		88" x 94"	Batting		96" x 114"

Directions are for both the double comforter and the queen coverlet. Information that differs for the queen coverlet is given in [ ].

Tip

- Scraps used to make *Wyoming Whirligig* are predominantly lavender, green, blue, and brown, with a few red sprinkled in. The prints are large- and small-scale florals, stripes, and plaids.
- Most blocks are made using just one scrap, while others are made with as many as four scraps that contain the same color. Choose the background fabric first; then select prints that contrast well with it.

Getting Started

Wash and press fabrics. Cut the patches and other pieces as listed in the materials and cutting box. Refer to page 92 for Quilting Basics.

Making the Blocks

1. Trace or photocopy 684 [924] of the foundation-piecing pattern.
2. Foundation-piece the fabric units in numerical order.
3. Make two halves for each block, but do not join them. Pair the block halves and set aside until making the rows.

Do not join

Block Piecing
Make 342 [462]

Assembling the Quilt Top

1. Join 19 [21] half blocks to make the first row, referring to row assembly on page 22.
2. To make the second row, pair every other half block with its mate in the first row. Set aside the remaining stack of half blocks to use in the last row. Fill in with new half blocks, again placing the leftover half blocks in a separate stack.
3. Join the rows.
4. To make the third row, pair the mates from the leftover stack from the second row with new half blocks in between.
5. Sew the third row to the second row.
6. Continue in this manner, making 32 [40] more rows of half blocks and joining them to the previous row when completed.
7. To make the last row, again pair mates, using the stack of half blocks from the first row as fillers. Join to the previous row.
8. Remove the paper.

Quilting and Finishing

1. Layer and baste the quilt backing, batting, and top.

2. Quilt in-the-ditch, extending the diagonal lines through the scrap patches.

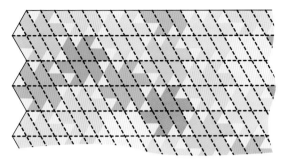

Quilting Placement

3. Trim quilt backing and batting even with the quilt top.
4. Make bias binding, referring to bias binding instructions on page 94.
5. Bind the quilt, referring to Binding and Hexagons.

Binding and Hexagons

The tricky part of applying binding to hexagon shapes is the corner folds. At the outer corners, backstitch, remove the needle, and position the binding along the next edge. At the inner corners, pivot and sew to the next edge in a continuous seam.

To get started, cut the beginning of the binding strip at a 45° angle. Fold under ¼" on this side and on one long side. Press. Pin the binding strip along one long edge of the quilt front. Sew from the fold to ¼" from the first corner of the quilt, backstitching at both ends.

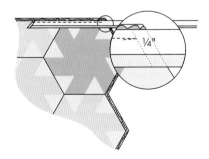

Lift the needle from the quilt and cut the threads. Fold the binding up.

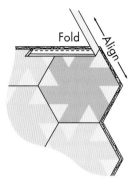

Fold the binding back down, matching raw edges. Sew just to the seamline in the middle of the block, backstitching at both ends.

Lift the needle from the quilt and cut the threads. Fold and pin the binding in place along the next edge. Beginning with backstitching, sew just to the seamline between the two blocks and stop with the needle down.

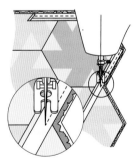

Turn the quilt, reposition the binding on the next edge, and continue sewing to the seam line in the middle of the next block. Backstitch. The fabric will ease into the inner point without an additional tuck.

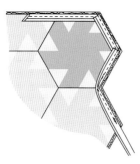

Repeat these steps around the perimeter of the quilt, stopping a few inches from the starting point.

Trim excess binding, leaving ample length to cover the fold at the beginning of the strip. Sew the end of the binding in place.

Turn the binding to the back of the quilt and blindstitch the binding to the backing, forming a small tuck at each outer corner.

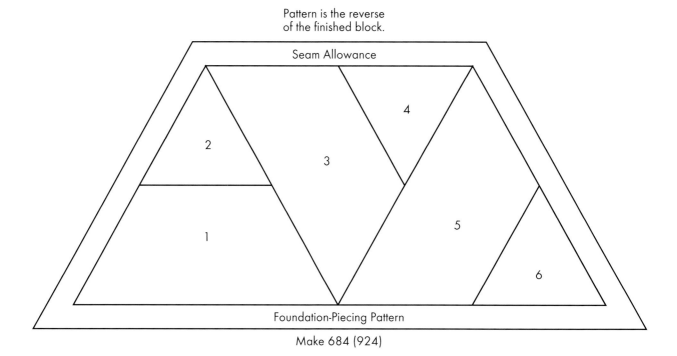

First 3 Rows

Last Row
Row Assembly

Double comforter is shown in darker colors.
Queen coverlet includes the complete diagram.

Pattern is the reverse
of the finished block.

Seam Allowance

2

4

3

1

5

6

Foundation-Piecing Pattern

Make 684 (924)

Keep the Home Fires Burning

INTERMEDIATE ◆◆

by Flavin Glover

Designed by Flavin Glover of Auburn, Alabama, *Keep the Home Fires Burning* was a twenty-fifth wedding anniversary gift for her husband, Glenn. The quilt was designed as a tribute to their first twenty-five years and a symbol for a continued life together. Selecting colors she thought her husband would enjoy viewing for many years to come, Flavin worked on the 71"-square quilt, on the sly, for more than a year.

Designed and made by Flavin Glover.

MATERIALS AND CUTTING

Quilt Size: 71" x 71"

Requirements are based on 42" fabric width.

Borders are the exact length required plus seam allowances.

Read all instructions before cutting. Cut foundation-piecing patches ¾" larger than pattern.

Materials	Yards	Cutting
Blue Print	2⅛ [1]	
inner borders (sides)		2 at 3½" x 55½"
inner borders (top/bottom)		2 at 3½" x 49½"
outer borders (sides)		2 at 1½" x 69½"
outer borders (top/bottom)		2 at 1½" x 71½"
Blue Solid	⅝	
binding		8 strips 2¼" x 42"
Tan Stripe	2[¾]	
short inner border (housetop)		1 at 1½" x 11"
short inner border (housetop)		1 at 1½" x 6"
inner borders (house bottom/sides)		3 at 1½" x 18"
outer borders (top/bottom/sides)		4 at 2½" x 65½"
Multi-Print	⅛	
borders (sides)		2 at 1¼" x 21½"
borders (top/bottom)		2 at 1¼" x 20"
Brown Check	¼	as needed for roof
Yellow/Gold Scraps	1½	as needed for house units Y and Z
		5 strips 1" x 36" for Rail Fence blocks
		12 strips 1¼" x 7½" for Rail Fence blocks
		as needed for blocks, edge, and corner triangles
quick piecing quarter-squares		2 bias strips each 3⅝" x 25", cut from each of two fabrics
or traditional piecing		56 A patches
		1½"-wide strips totaling 90" for Four-Patch centers
quick piecing quarter-squares		* 12 bias strips 3⅛" x 22"
or traditional piecing		* 96 E patches
Red Scraps	2⅝	as needed for house units Y and Z
		4 at 2½" x 2½"
		4 at 1½" x 1½"
		as needed for blocks, edge, and corner triangles
quick piecing quarter-squares		2 bias strips 3⅝" x 25", cut from each of two fabrics
or traditional piecing		40 A patches
		1½"-wide strips totaling 30" for Four-Patch centers
quick piecing quarter-squares		* 14 bias strips 3⅛" x 22"
or traditional piecing		* 112 E patches
		scraps for B, C, D patches
Purple Scraps	1	as needed for blocks

Materials	Yards	Cutting
Purple Scraps (continued)		
quick piecing quarter-squares		2 bias strips 3⅝" x 25", cut from each of two fabrics
or traditional piecing		40 A patches
quick piecing quarter-squares		* 3 bias strips 3⅛" x 22"
or traditional piecing		* 24 E patches
Blue Scraps	2	as needed for blocks
		24 strips 1¼" x 7½" for Rail Fence blocks
quick piecing quarter-squares		2 bias strips 3⅝" x 25", cut from each of two fabrics
or traditional piecing		56 A patches
		1½"-wide strips totaling 30" for Four-Patch centers
quick piecing quarter-squares		* 13 bias strips 3⅛" x 22"
or traditional piecing		* 104 E patches
		scraps for B, C, D patches
Green Scraps	2	as needed for blocks
		5 strips 1" x 18" for Rail Fence blocks
		8 strips 1¼" x 7½" for Rail Fence blocks
		as needed for edge and corner triangles
		1½"-wide strips totaling 30" for Four-Patch centers
quick piecing quarter-squares		* 6 bias strips 3⅛" x 22"
or traditional piecing		* 48 E patches
		scraps for B, C, D patches
Brown Scraps	¼	as needed for blocks (chimney) (2" x 1½")
		5 strips 1" x 18" for Rail Fence blocks
		4 strips 1¼" x 7½" for Rail Fence blocks
Backing	4⅜	2 panels 38" x 75"
Batting		75" x 75"

Yardage given in [ ] is for pieced borders cut crosswise.

*The number of strips is approximate, based on the balance of color in the designer's quilt. Those making this quilt may choose a different combination of colors in the Pinwheel blocks.

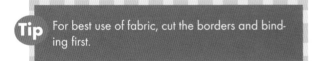

Tip For best use of fabric, cut the borders and binding first.

Getting Started

Wash and press fabrics. Cut the patches and other pieces as listed in the materials and cutting box. Refer to page 92 for Quilting Basics.

Making the Blocks and Assembling the Quilt Top

Center House Blocks

1. Trace or photocopy ten unit Y and five unit Z.
2. Foundation-piece the fabric units in numerical order.
3. Make ten unit Y and five unit Z, referring to row diagrams for color placement and noting that unit Y has six different colorations and unit Z has three. In some of the blocks, patches 1A,

1B, 1C, and 1D are all pieced, while in other blocks 1A–1D are combined so that only one fabric patch is needed. In the units in row 2, patches 1A–1C are combined into one patch and 1D is a separate patch.

House Row 1 Units

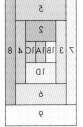 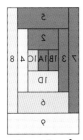  

Front
Unit Y - Make 1

Front Roof
Unit Y - Make 1

Roof
Unit Y - Make 2

Back Roof
Unit Y - Make 1

House Row 2 Units

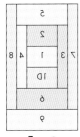 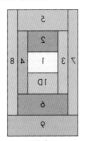

Front
Unit Y - Make 2

Side
Unit Y - Make 3

House Row 3 Units

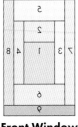 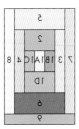 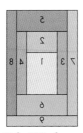

Front Window
Unit Z - Make 1

Door
Unit Z - Make 1

Side Windows
Unit Z - Make 3

To aid in fabric placement, note that the unit diagrams are shown from the finished or fabric side, not from the sewing side.

4. Appliqué a favorite cat shape in windows, if desired.
5. Join the blocks in three rows of five blocks each, referring to the partial quilt assembly—part 1. Press seam allowances in opposite directions.

• = Chimney Patch

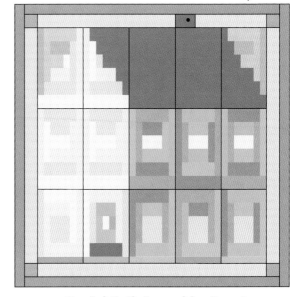

Partial Quilt Assembly - Part 1

6. Join the rows. Press seam allowances in one direction.
7. Remove the paper.
8. Sew the short, inner tan-stripe borders to the chimney patch and sew the assembled border to the top of the house.
9. Sew one long, inner tan-stripe border to the bottom of the house.
10. Sew red 1½" squares to ends of remaining tan-stripe inner borders. Sew borders to the sides of the house.
11. Sew short, multi-print borders to the top and bottom. Sew long, multi-print borders to the sides.

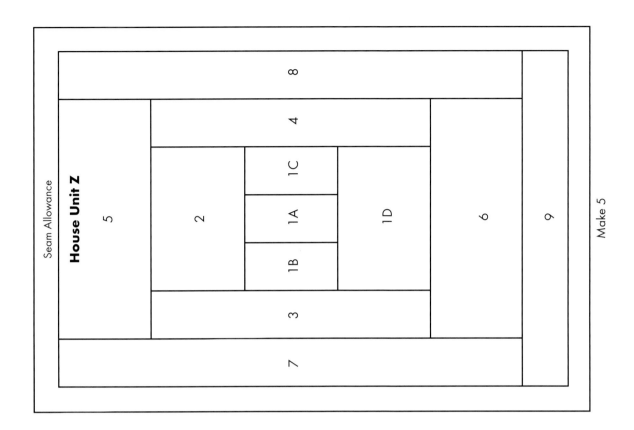

House Unit Z

Seam Allowance

Make 5

Patterns are the reverse of the finished block.

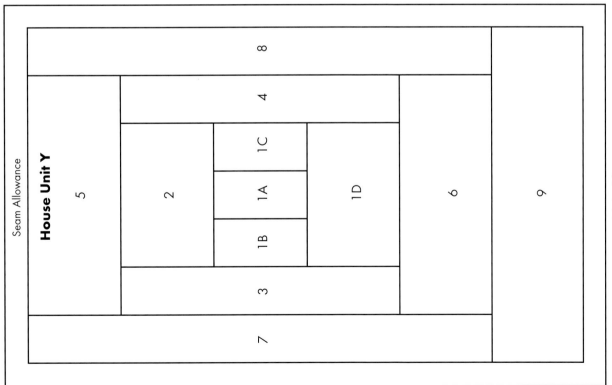

House Unit Y

Seam Allowance

Make 10

Log Cabin Stars and Rail Fence Border

1. Trace or photocopy eight Log Cabin star centers, sixteen side star points, and sixteen top star points.

2. Foundation-piece the fabric units in numerical order.

3. Make eight Log Cabin star centers, sixteen side star points, and sixteen top star points, referring to photo for color placement. Note that there are three yellow stars and two green stars with a blue background, two red stars and one purple star with a green background.

4. Sew the star points to the Log Cabin centers, referring to star block piecing.

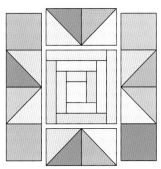

Star Block Piecing
Make 8

5. Remove the paper.

6. To strip piece the Rail Fence blocks, sew five 1"-wide yellow strips together lengthwise to make a yellow band. Repeat with 1"-wide green strips and 1"-wide brown strips. When assembled, each band should measure 3" wide from raw edge to raw edge.

7. Press seam allowances in one direction.

Strip Piecing

8. Cut eight 2¾"-wide units and four 3"-wide units from the yellow band, four 2¾"-wide and two 3"-wide units from the brown band, and four 2¾"-wide and two 3"-wide units from the green band.

9. Sew the 1¼" x 7½" strips together in sets of three. Make twelve blue/yellow/blue pieced sets and four green/brown/green pieced sets.

10. Join the units and the pieced sets to make the blocks in the color combinations shown, referring to Rail Fence blocks piecing.

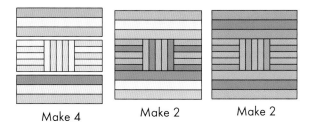

Make 4   Make 2   Make 2

Rail Fence Blocks Piecing

11. Join Rail Fence blocks with star blocks to make the top and bottom borders, referring to partial quilt assembly—part 2.

12. Sew the borders to the top and bottom of the center house block.

13. Join the remaining Rail Fence blocks with star blocks to make the side borders, referring to partial quilt assembly—part 2.

14. Sew the borders to the sides of the center house block.

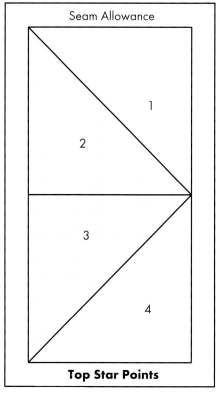

Top Star Points

Make 16

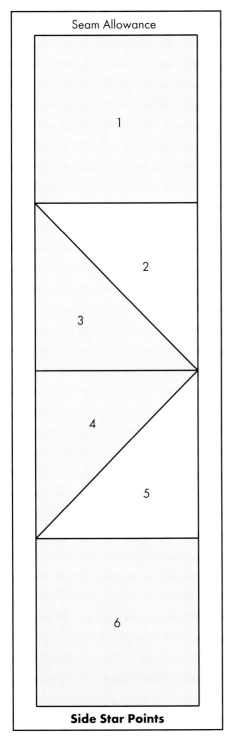

Seam Allowance

1

2

3

4

5

6

Side Star Points

Make 16

Partial Quilt Assembly - Part 2

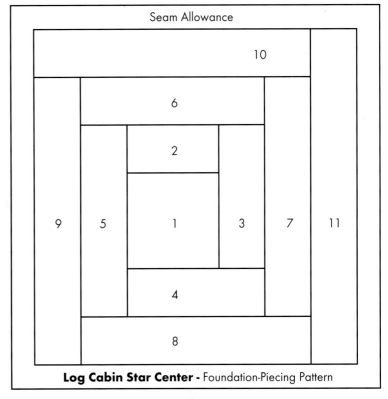

Seam Allowance

10

6

2

9   5   1   3   7   11

4

8

Log Cabin Star Center - Foundation-Piecing Pattern

Make 8

Middle Border

1. Trace or photocopy forty-eight little log cabins, sixteen corner triangles, and forty edge triangles.

2. Foundation-piece the little log cabins in numerical order.

3. Make forty-eight little log cabins in colors desired. The designer made fourteen red, ten gold, fourteen purple, and ten blue.

4. Make forty-eight quarter-square triangle units, using traditional piecing methods with A patches or referring to the quick method on page 31. The designer made ten red, fourteen gold, ten purple, and fourteen blue quarter-square triangle units.

5. Join two little log cabins with two quarter-square triangles to make a block, referring to block piecing.

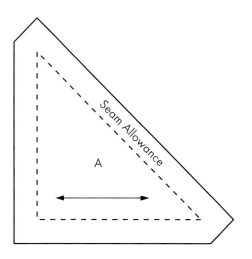

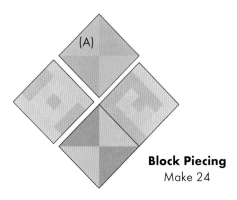

Block Piecing
Make 24

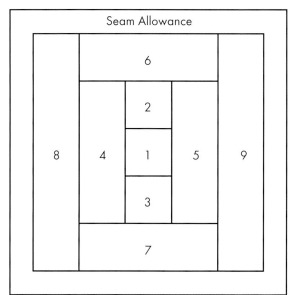

Little Log Cabin - Foundation-Piecing Pattern
Make 48

6. Foundation-piece corner triangles and edge triangles in numerical order.

7. Make twenty red edge triangles, twenty green edge triangles, eight red corner triangles, and eight green corner triangles.

8. Join the blocks, edge triangles, and corner triangles to make the side borders, referring to partial quilt assembly—part 3.

9. Sew the borders to the sides.

10. Join the blocks, edge triangles, and corner triangles to make the top and bottom borders.

11. Sew the borders to the top and bottom.

12. Sew the 3 1/2"-wide blue borders to the top and bottom. Sew the 3 1/2"-wide blue borders to the sides.

Partial Quilt Assembly - Part 3

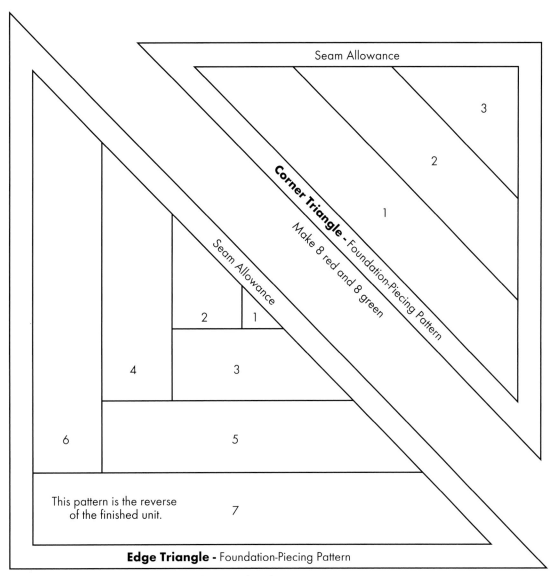

Seam Allowance

3

2

1

Corner Triangle - Foundation-Piecing Pattern

Make 8 red and 8 green

Seam Allowance

2 | 1

4 | 3

6 | 5

This pattern is the reverse
of the finished unit.

7

Edge Triangle - Foundation-Piecing Pattern

Make 20 red and 20 green

Quarter-Square Triangles

Following is a quick method for making the quarter-square triangle units, which are used in the blocks in the middle border. Each unit is made using two colors that are close in value. Select two reds, two golds, two purples, and two blues. From each fabric, cut two $3\frac{5}{8}$" x 25" bias strips. Join the four strips. Press seam allowances in one direction. Use a square rotary ruler that has a 45° line marked along the diagonal. Line up the diagonal mark with the first seam. Cut $3\frac{3}{8}$" squares from the bands. Cut the two-color squares in half diagonally. Join two triangles to make each unit. Make forty-eight units. Repeat with golds, purples, and blues.

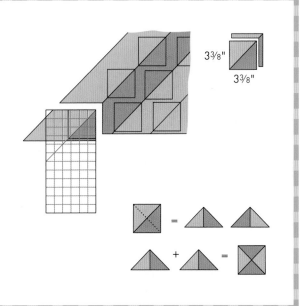

$3\frac{3}{8}$"

$3\frac{3}{8}$"

Outer Border

1. Trace or photocopy twenty-four Log Cabin blocks.
2. To make the Four-Patch centers, sew 1¹⁄₂"-wide gold strips to 1¹⁄₂"-wide blue, green, or red strips the same length to make pieced bands.
3. Press the seam allowances away from the gold strips.
4. Cut the bands into forty-eight 1¹⁄₂"-wide segments.
5. Join two segments to make a Four-Patch center.

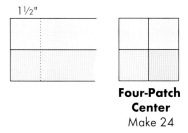

Four-Patch Center
Make 24

6. Position and pin a Four-Patch center in the middle of a paper foundation in #1 patch position. Sew strips around the center in numerical order to make Log Cabin blocks. Note that half of each block is made with red logs and the other half is made with either blue or green logs.
7. Remove the paper.
8. To make Pinwheel blocks, use either the traditional piecing - or the quick-piecing method.
9. If using the traditional-piecing method, trace or photocopy 384 E patches, referring to quilt photo for color ideas. Join E patches with B, C, and D patches, referring to Pinwheel block piecing.

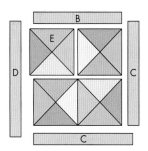

Pinwheel Block Piecing
Make 24

10. If using the quick-piecing method, refer to Quarter-Square Triangles instructions on page 31. Join 3¹⁄₈" x 22" bias strips to make a band. Fabric Tip: Sew yellow/gold strips alternately with red, blue, green, and purple strips to make one band. Then sew the remaining red, blue, green, and purple strips into bands, arranging colors for a scrappy look, to make a second band. Cut the bands into 2⁷⁄₈" squares, referring to Quarter-Square Triangles instructions on page 31. Cut the squares in half diagonally to make units. Arrange the units into blocks, referring to Pinwheel block piecing. Sew B, C, and D patches to the edges.
11. Join the Log Cabin blocks and the Pinwheel blocks alternately to make the side borders, referring to quilt assembly—complete.
12. Sew the borders to the sides.
13. Join the Log Cabin blocks and the Pinwheel blocks alternately to make the top and bottom borders, referring to quilt assembly—complete.
14. Sew the borders to the top and bottom.
15. Sew the 2¹⁄₂"-wide tan stripe outer borders to the sides.
16. Sew red 2¹⁄₂" squares to the ends of the remaining tan stripe outer borders. Sew borders to the top and bottom.
17. Sew blue borders to the sides. Sew blue borders to the top and bottom. Press the seam allowances toward the borders.

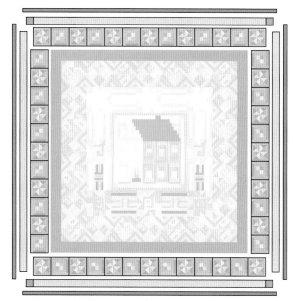

Quilt Assembly - Complete

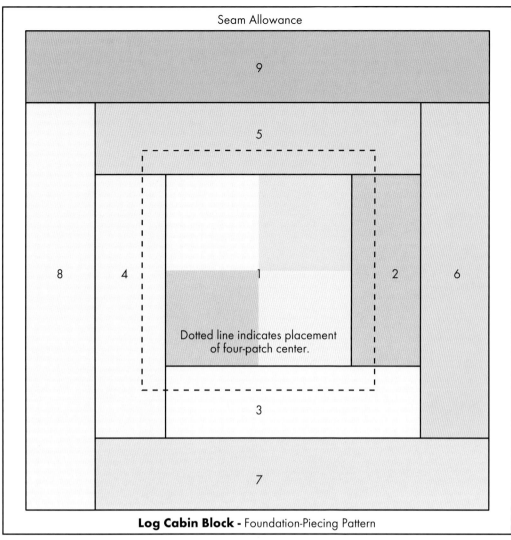

Seam Allowance

9

5

8　　4　　1　　2　　6

Dotted line indicates placement
of four-patch center.

3

7

Log Cabin Block - Foundation-Piecing Pattern

Make 24

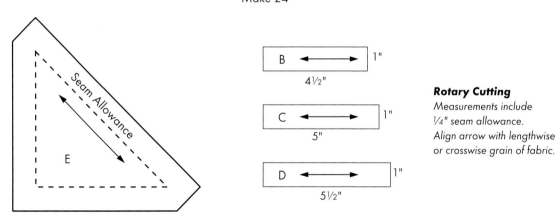

Seam Allowance

E

B ⟷ 1"
4½"

C ⟷ 1"
5"

D ⟷ 1"
5½"

Rotary Cutting
*Measurements include
¼" seam allowance.
Align arrow with lengthwise
or crosswise grain of fabric.*

Quilting and Finishing

1. Mark each 3½"-wide blue border with desired quilting design before layering and basting.
2. Layer and baste the quilt backing, batting, and top.
3. Quilt the marked lines and in-the-ditch around the patches.
4. Trim quilt backing and batting even with the quilt top.
5. Join 2¼"-wide strips diagonally to make the binding. Bind the quilt.

Goldfinch & Thistle

by Brenda Groelz

INTERMEDIATE ◆◆

Brenda Groelz, the designer of *Goldfinch & Thistle*, notes that she has always been drawn to pictorial quilts, but that finding patterns for piecing pictures that aren't stylized or primitive can be difficult. Combining piecing with pictures is her passion. She notes that her goal as a pattern designer is to enable the maker of a pieced quilt to create the same realism achieved by quiltmakers who use appliqué. Piecing on foundations allows the accuracy that these small pieces and sharp angles demand.

Designed and made by Brenda Groelz.

MATERIALS AND CUTTING

Block Size:		7" x 10"
Quilt Size:		12½" x 15½"

Requirements are based on 42" fabric width.

Borders are the exact length required plus seam allowances.

Read all instructions before cutting. Cut foundation-piecing patches ¾" larger than pattern.

Materials	Yards	Cutting
Assorted Fabric Scraps		bird and thistle
Green Print	¼	1 each A, B, C, D, background patches
Black Print	⅛	
inner borders (sides)		2 at 1½" x 10½"
inner borders (top/bottom)		2 at 1½" x 9½"
Medium Purple Print	¼	
outer borders (sides)		2 at 2¼" x 12½"
outer borders (top/bottom)		2 at 2¼" x 13"
Dark Purple Print	¼	
binding		2 strips 2¼" x 42"
Backing	½	
backing		1 panel 15" x 18"
sleeve		9" x 12½"
Batting		17" x 20"

Supplies: Black embroidery floss

Tip

- Using a non-directional print for the green fabric will help hide the seams in the background around the bird and the thistle.
- A solid or a tone-on-tone fabric will work well for the small pieces in the goldfinch, and a narrow black-and-white stripe will work best for the tips of the wings.
- To create the chevron effect in the goldfinch's wing tips, sew the black-and-white striped fabric so that its lines follow the printed lines on blocks S and T.
- Let imagination lead the way when considering prints for *Goldfinch & Thistle*, as the perfect texture may be hiding in an unlikely fabric. When cut into small pieces, the petals or leaves of a floral print might look like feathers. A geometric print might make the thistle appear prickly. Another texture may even transform the thistle into another flower.

Getting Started

Wash and press fabrics. Cut the patches and other pieces as listed in the materials and cutting box. Refer to page 92 for Quilting Basics.

Making the Blocks

1. Trace or photocopy one each of blocks P–Z.
2. Foundation-piece the fabric units in numerical order.

Assembling the Quilt Top

1. Sew the foundation-pieced blocks and A–D patches in horizontal rows, referring to quilt assembly.

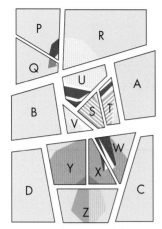

Quilt Assembly

2. Join the rows.
3. Sew the inner borders to the sides of the quilt. Sew the inner borders to the top and bottom. Press the seam allowances toward the borders.
4. Sew the outer borders to the sides of the quilt. Sew the outer borders to the top and bottom. Press the seam allowances toward the borders.
5. Remove the paper.
6. Satin stitch the goldfinch's eye.

Satin Stitch

Quilting and Finishing

1. Freehand mark the quilting lines on the blocks and borders.
2. Layer and baste the quilt backing, batting, and top.
3. Quilt along marked quilting lines.
4. Trim quilt backing and batting even with the quilt top.
5. Join 2¼"-wide strips diagonally to make the binding. Bind the quilt.

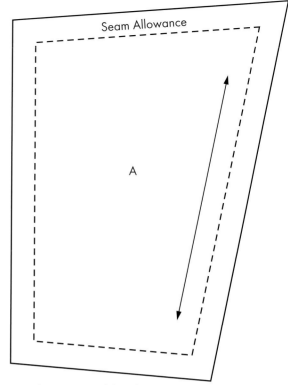

Align arrows with lengthwise or crosswise grain of fabric.

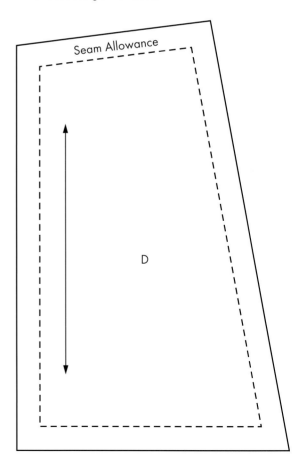

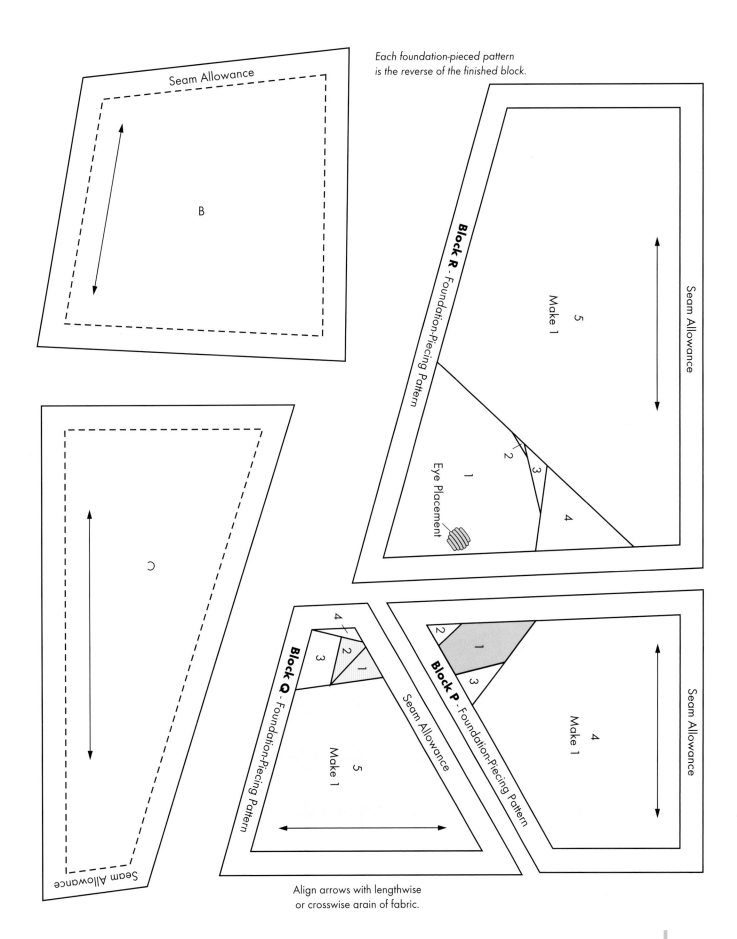

Each foundation-pieced pattern is the reverse of the finished block.

Seam Allowance

B

Seam Allowance

C

Seam Allowance

Block R - Foundation-Piecing Pattern

Seam Allowance

5
Make 1

Eye Placement

1

2

3

4

Block Q - Foundation-Piecing Pattern

4

2

3

1

5
Make 1

Seam Allowance

Block P - Foundation-Piecing Pattern

2

1

3

4
Make 1

Seam Allowance

Align arrows with lengthwise
or crosswise grain of fabric.

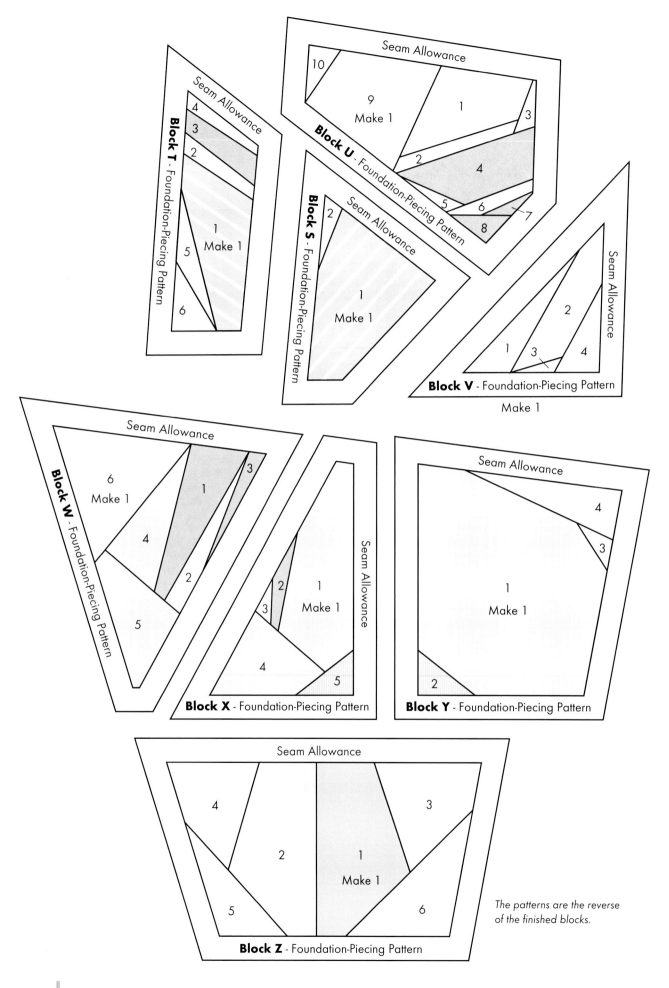

Block T - Foundation-Piecing Pattern

Seam Allowance

4
3
2
1
Make 1
5
6

Block U - Foundation-Piecing Pattern

Seam Allowance

10
9
Make 1
1
3
2
4
5
6
7
8

Block S - Foundation-Piecing Pattern

Seam Allowance

2
1
Make 1

Block V - Foundation-Piecing Pattern

Seam Allowance

2
1
3
4

Make 1

Block W - Foundation-Piecing Pattern

Seam Allowance

6
Make 1
3
1
4
2
5

Block X - Foundation-Piecing Pattern

Seam Allowance

2
3
1
Make 1
4
5

Block Y - Foundation-Piecing Pattern

Seam Allowance

4
3
1
Make 1
2

Block Z - Foundation-Piecing Pattern

Seam Allowance

4
2
1
Make 1
3
5
6

The patterns are the reverse of the finished blocks.

Nancy's Garden

INTERMEDIATE ◆◇ *by Liz Schwartz and Stephen Seifert*

What do a trained biologist and someone with a degree in English literature and psychology have in common? Both are self-taught quilters who, since discovering foundation piecing, have used this technique exclusively to create their designs, including the stained glass *Nancy's Garden*. Liz Schwartz, the biologist, and Stephen Seifert began quilting seriously in 1992, learning on traditional patterns and then moving to more-contemporary designs.

Designed and made by Liz Schwartz and Stephen Seifert. Quilted by Grace Karnes.

MATERIALS AND CUTTING

Block Size: 6"

Quilt Size: 48" x 48"

Requirements are based on 42" fabric width.

Borders are the exact length required plus seam allowances.

Read all instructions before cutting. Cut foundation-piecing patches ¾" larger than pattern

Materials	Yards	Cutting
Black Solid	4	
binding		3 strips 2¼" x 71"
borders		4 at 6½" x 36½"
		1"-wide strips for stained glass leading blocks
Gold Solid	3/8	20 #1 patches for Z blocks
Orange Solid	3/8	20 #15 patches for Z blocks
Light Blue Solid	3/8	20 #13 patches for Y blocks
Medium Light Blue Solid	3/8	20 #9 patches for Y blocks
Light Green Solid	3/8	20 #3 patches for Y blocks
Medium Light Green Solid	3/8	20 #9 patches for Z blocks
Tan Solid	5/8	20 #1 patches for Y blocks; 20 #7 patches for Z blocks
Medium Blue Solid	1/2	20 each #6, 7 patches for Y blocks
Gray Solid	5/8	20 each #13, 14 patches for Z blocks
Pink Solid	1	20 each #14, 15 patches for Y blocks
		20 each #5, 6 patches for Z blocks
Backing	3⅛	
backing		2 panels 27" x 52"
sleeve		9" x 48"
Batting		52" x 52"

Tip
- To closely replicate the look of stained glass, look for batiks, hand-dyed, or commercially printed tone-on-tone prints with a marbled appearance.
- Cut the binding and border strips from the black fabric first. Then cut remaining black fabric into 1"-wide strips for easy-to-sew "stained-glass leading."
- This design is also striking made with fabrics of medium and dark values.

Getting Started

Wash and press fabrics. Cut the patches and other pieces as listed in the materials and cutting box. Refer to page 92 for Quilting Basics.

Making the Blocks

1. Trace or photocopy twenty of the Y block, twenty of the Z block section 1, and twenty of the Z block section 2.

2. Foundation-piece the fabric units in numerical order.

Block Y Piecing
Make 20

Block Z Piecing
Make 20

3. Join the Z block sections to form twenty Z blocks. Press Z block seam allowances open to reduce bulk.

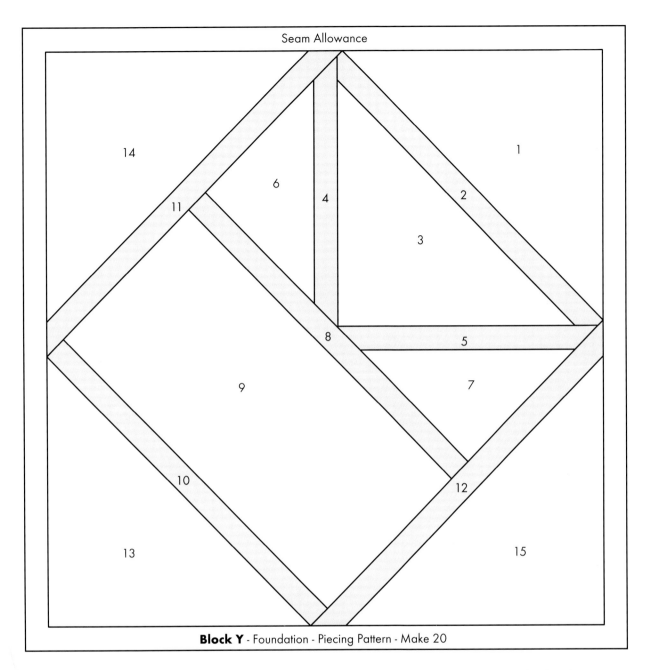

Seam Allowance

14

1

6

4

11

2

3

8

5

9

7

10

12

13

15

Block Y - Foundation - Piecing Pattern - Make 20

Assembling the Quilt Top

1. Join the Y and Z blocks, referring to row assembly. Press the seam allowances open to reduce bulk.

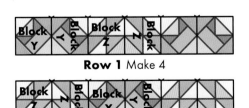

Row 1 Make 4

Row 2 Make 2
Row Assembly

2. Join a Z block to each end of a border strip, orienting the Z blocks as shown. Press the seam allowances open to reduce bulk.

Top/Bottom Border Make 2

3. Join the rows, referring to quilt assembly. Quilt assembly shows half of the quilt top. Make two

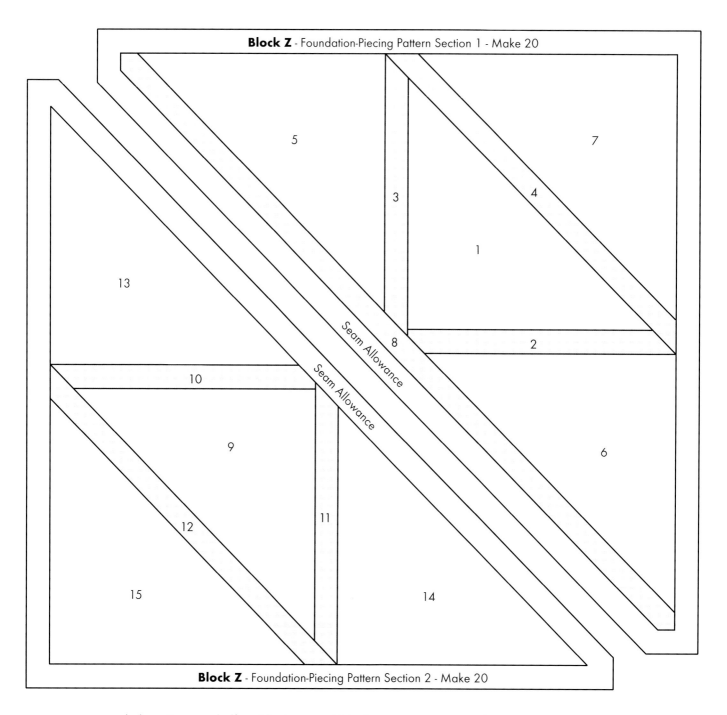

Block Z - Foundation-Piecing Pattern Section 1 - Make 20

Seam Allowance

Seam Allowance

Block Z - Foundation-Piecing Pattern Section 2 - Make 20

halves. Turn one half upside down and join the halves.

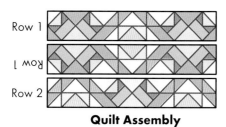

Quilt Assembly

4. Sew the borders to the sides of the quilt. Sew the top and bottom borders to the top and bottom. Press the seam allowances toward the borders.

5. Remove the paper.

Quilting and Finishing

1. Layer and baste the quilt backing, batting, and top.
2. Quilt all the black patches in-the-ditch, extending the lines into the border.
3. Trim quilt backing and batting even with the quilt top.
4. Join 2¼"-wide strips diagonally to make the binding. Bind the quilt.
5. Sew a sleeve to the backing for display purposes.

Drake Lake

by Rebecca Manthey

INTERMEDIATE ◆◆

Designer Rebecca Manthey created *Drake Lake* for a friend who wanted a homemade quilt. At the time, she wanted pictures as opposed to geometric shapes, but she couldn't find many "guy" patterns. The recipient is an avid duck hunter, so a duck quilt was the obvious choice.

Designed by Rebecca Manthey. Sewn by Lucy Brown. Quilted by Maria Capp.

Tip *Drake Lake* uses six different color combinations for the ducks, as shown on page 44. Each of the duck blocks has four sections to foundation piece. The dotted lines indicate where to piece additional patches according to the duck species. For instance, the Mallard Drake has an additional fabric sewn on the head to create a collar (4b patch).

Getting Started

Wash and press fabrics. Cut the patches and other pieces as listed in the materials and cutting box. Refer to page 92 for Quilting Basics.

Making the Blocks

1. Trace or photocopy 9 [30] of the Y block and 6 [29] of the Z block.
2. For each Y block, foundation-piece the fabric units in numerical order.
3. For each Z block, foundation-piece the fabric units in numerical order, piecing in sections 1–4. Refer to Z block piecing for appropriate fabric placement for the six different species and appropriate number of each species to

MATERIALS AND CUTTING

Block Sizes: 6"x 6", 6" x 9"

Quilt Sizes: Wall Quilt (shown), [Twin Comforter]   40" x 25" [66" x 87"]

Requirements are based on 42" fabric width.

Borders are the exact length required plus seam allowances.

Read all instructions before cutting. Cut foundation-piecing patches ¾" larger than pattern.

Materials	Yards	Cutting	Materials	Yards	Cutting
Wall Quilt			**Twin Comforter**		
Blue Print	1 7/8		Blue Print	5½	
outer borders (sides)		2 at 2½" x 21½"	sash 1		9 strips 2" x 35"
outer borders (top/bottom)		2 at 2½" x 40½"	sash 2		56 strips 2" x 6½"
sash 1		2 strips 2" x 36½"	foundation-piecing		background patches
sash 2		none for this size	Green Print	3	
foundation-piecing		background patches	inner borders (sides)		2 at 5¾" x 68"
Green Print	1/3		inner border (bottom)		1 at 5" x 45½"
inner borders (sides)		none for this size	outer borders (sides)		2 at 5" x 78½"
inner borders (top/bottom)		none for this size	outer borders (top/bottom)		2 at 5" x 66½"
binding		4 strips 2¼" x 42"	binding		9 strips 2¼" x 42"
Assorted Fabric Scraps			Assorted Fabric Scraps		
foundation-piecing		ducks, grass blades	foundation-piecing		ducks, grass blades
Backing	1 3/8		Backing	5¼	
backing		1 panel 29" x 44"	backing		2 panels 36" x 91"
sleeve		9" x 40"	sleeve		none for this size
Batting		29" x 44"	Batting		70" x 91"

Supplies: Black embroidery floss or 6 [29] black ⅜" buttons

Directions are for both the wall quilt and the twin comforter. Information that differs for the twin comforter is given in [ ].

make for each size quilt. Join Z block sections, referring to Z block piecing.

Mallard Drake
Make 1 [2]

Cinnamon Teal
Make 1 [6]

Mallard Hen
Make 1 [8]

Redhead
Make 1 [6]

Blue-winged Teal
Make 1 [3]

Scaup
Make 1 [4]

Block Z Piecing

4. Press seam allowances open between the sections.

Assembling the Quilt Top

1. Join three Y blocks and two Z blocks to make a row, referring to wall quilt assembly for block placement. Make three rows as shown. [Join two Y blocks and two Z blocks with four sash 2 strips to make a row, referring to twin comforter assembly for block and sash placement. Make nine rows as shown.]

2. Join the rows and sash 1 strips, alternating as shown in wall quilt assembly. [Join the rows and sash 1 strips, alternating as shown in twin comforter assembly].

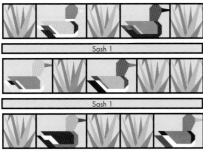

Wall Quilt Assembly

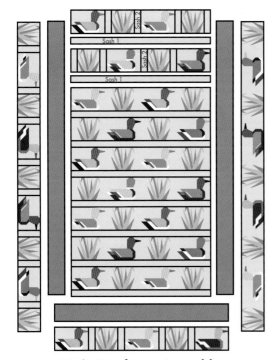

Twin Comforter Assembly

3. Sew the borders to the sides of the quilt. Sew the borders to the top and bottom. Press the seam allowances toward the borders. [Sew the borders to the sides of the quilt. Sew the border to the bottom. Join three Z blocks, two Y blocks, and four sash 2 strips to make a bottom, pieced border. Join four Z blocks, five Y blocks, and eight sash 2 strips to make a side, pieced border. Make two side, pieced borders. Sew pieced border to the bottom of the quilt. Sew pieced borders to the sides of the quilt.]

4. Remove the paper.

5. Satin stitch the duck's eye on each Z block or sew on a black button for eye as indicated on foundation-piecing pattern.

Satin Stitch

Quilting and Finishing

1. Layer and baste the quilt backing, batting, and top.

2. Quilt in-the-ditch around the grass and duck shapes. Remaining areas can be free-form quilted in a water-current pattern, as shown in photo, or can be quilted with straight lines as shown in the twin comforter quilting placement. Parallel lines in the borders are spaced 1½" apart.

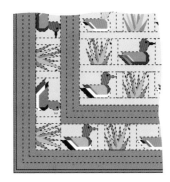

Twin Comforter Quilting Placement

3. Trim quilt backing and batting even with the quilt top.

4. Join 2¼"-wide strips diagonally to make the binding. Bind the quilt.

5. Sew a sleeve to the backing for display purposes.

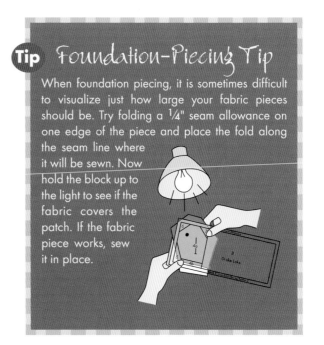

Tip Foundation-Piecing Tip

When foundation piecing, it is sometimes difficult to visualize just how large your fabric pieces should be. Try folding a ¼" seam allowance on one edge of the piece and place the fold along the seam line where it will be sewn. Now hold the block up to the light to see if the fabric covers the patch. If the fabric piece works, sew it in place.

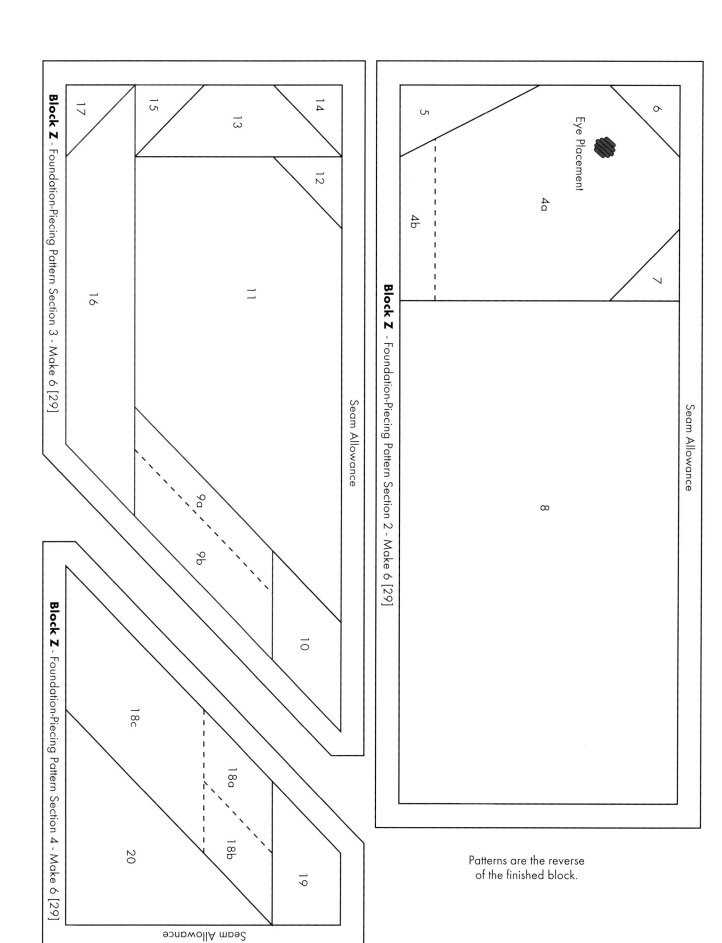

Block Z - Foundation-Piecing Pattern Section 2 - Make 6 [29]

Eye Placement

6

5

4b

4a

7

8

Seam Allowance

Patterns are the reverse
of the finished block.

Block Z - Foundation-Piecing Pattern Section 3 - Make 6 [29]

14

13

12

15

17

16

11

10

9a

9b

Seam Allowance

Block Z - Foundation-Piecing Pattern Section 4 - Make 6 [29]

18c

18a

18b

20

19

Seam Allowance

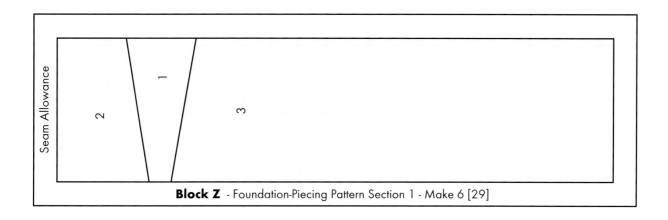

Block Z - Foundation-Piecing Pattern Section 1 - Make 6 [29]

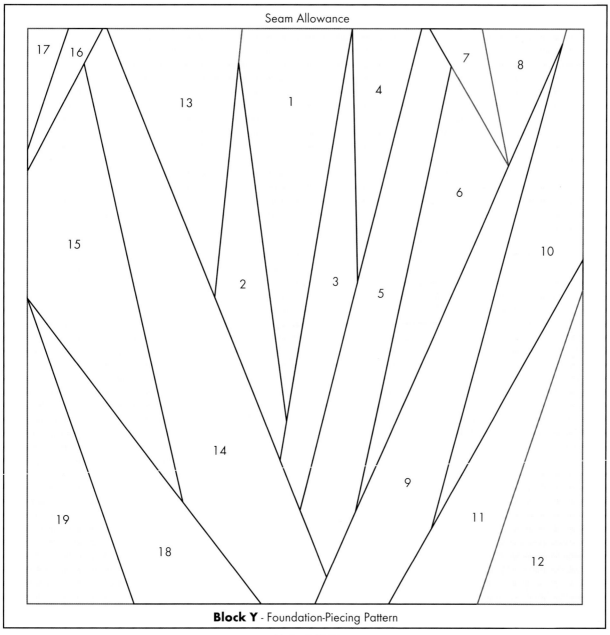

Block Y - Foundation-Piecing Pattern

Make 9 [30]

Folk Art Compass

INTERMEDIATE ◆◆

By Chris Taricani

Appliquéd hearts, easy-to-piece compasses, and multiple borders fit together to make this charming folk-art quilt, which won first place in the 1996 Hoffman Challenge. An interesting sampler of patterns, this quilt would be a good learning tool for quiltmakers with some experience who wish to master new techniques.

Designed and made by Chris Taricani.

MATERIALS AND CUTTING

Block Sizes: 7" x 7", 11" x 11"

Quilt Size: 35" x 35"

Requirements are based on 42" fabric width.

Borders are the exact length required plus seam allowances.

Read all instructions before cutting. Cut foundation-piecing patches ¾" larger than pattern.

Materials	Yards	Cutting
White Solid	1½	8 F, 16 I patches
middle borders		2 at 1⅛" x 27½"; 2 at 1⅛" x 26¼"
outer borders		2 at 1½" x 35½"; 2 at 1½" x 33½"
foundation-piecing		8 each #1, 3, 4 patches for unit Y;
		8 each #1, 3, 4 patches for unit Z
checkerboard borders		1½"-wide strips made from leftover fabric
White Stripe/Plaid	scraps	
foundation-piecing		8 #6 patches for unit Y
appliqué		16 reduced E stars (optional)
Tan Print	¾	4 B, 48 C patches
		20 each #2, 3 patches for unit X
Gold Print	¼	4 each E stars, H patches
appliqué		1 sun face (optional)
inner borders		2 at 1⅛" x 25"; 2 at 1⅛" x 26¼"
Striped Print #1	⅛	
center compass border		1 at 1½" x 13½"
Striped Print #2	⅛	
center compass border		1 at 1½" x 13½"
Striped Print #3	⅛	
center compass border		1 at 1½" x 13½"
Striped Print #4	⅛	
center compass border		1 at 1½" x 13½"
Leftover Striped Prints #1, 2, 3, 4		
binding		2¼" x 4¼ yards
Red/White/Blue Scraps	⅝	
foundation-piecing		20 each #1, 4 patches for unit X, 8G hearts
checkerboard borders		1½"-wide strips made from leftover fabric
Red Scraps	¼	
foundation-piecing		8 #7 patches for unit Y
Blue Scraps	⅜	1 A, 48 C, 4 D, 4 J patches
foundation-piecing		8 each #2, 5 patches for unit Y
		8 #2 patches for unit Z
Backing	1⅛	1 panel 39" x 39"
Batting		39" x 39"

- The designer used fabrics with uneven stripes for some of the borders and the binding, a flag print for the outer pieced border squares, a blue print with white stars for the center compass, and a sun print for the center circle. Because it may be difficult to find the same or similar fabrics, embroidered and appliquéd motifs have been included. These motifs can take the place of some of the fabric motifs, allowing re-creations of this quilt to keep the folk-art look of the original.
- Before cutting the patches for the small compasses, look closely at the compasses and note how the fabric prints were cut to add movement and interest to the blocks.

Getting Started

Wash and press fabrics. Cut the patches and other pieces as listed in the materials and cutting box. Refer to page 92 for Quilting Basics.

Making the Blocks

Center Compass and Sawtooth Border Block

1. Trace or photocopy eight Y units and eight Z units.
2. Foundation-piece the fabric units in numerical order.
3. Join one Y unit with one Z unit to make a compass section.
4. Make eight compass sections.
5. Join the eight compass sections to make the compass.
6. Appliqué the A patch over the raw edges in the center of the compass.
7. Use permanent markers to draw the sun face on a gold fabric circle, if desired. Then sew the sun patch to the A patch, using a Blanket stitch.

Blanket Stitch

8. Remove the paper.
9. Sew the B patches to the compass, referring to center compass assembly and aligning the narrow points of the compass with the dots on the B patches.

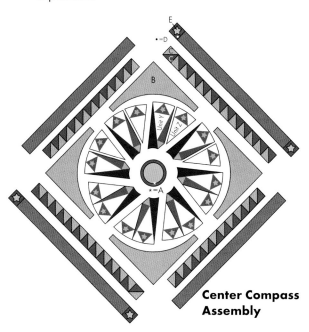

Center Compass Assembly

10. Join the B patches where their short ends meet to complete the block.
11. Join blue and tan C patches in pairs to make forty-eight two-color squares.
12. Join eleven squares. Sew to one side of the compass block, referring to center compass assembly. Repeat for the opposite side.
13. Join thirteen squares, rotating the end squares as shown in center compass assembly. Sew to one side of the compass block. Repeat for the remaining side.
14. Sew the inner borders to the sides of the block, referring to center compass assembly.
15. Sew a D patch to each end of the remaining inner borders. Sew the borders to the remaining sides of the block.
16. Appliqué, fuse, or embroider an E star to each D patch.
17. Reduce the E star to 75% and add one small E star to all #2 patches in Y and Z units, if desired.

Small Compass Blocks and Appliqué Hearts

1. Trace or photocopy twenty X units.
2. Foundation-piece the fabric units in numerical order.
3. Join five X units to make a small compass.
4. Appliqué the H patch over the raw edges in the center of the compass.
5. Remove the paper.
6. Sew the I patches to the compass, referring to small compass piecing and orienting the five-pointed star within the I patches as shown.

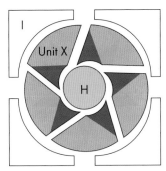

Small Compass Piecing

7. Join the I patches where their short ends meet to complete the block.
8. Make four small compass blocks.
9. Sew two F patches to a small compass block, joining the pieces along the short edges of the F patches and properly orienting the star. Refer to partial quilt assembly.

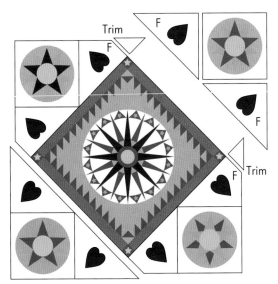

Partial Quilt Assembly

10. Repeat for remaining small compass blocks to make compass units.
11. Sew a compass unit to one side of the center compass and sawtooth border block, matching the centers and trimming the ends even with the edges of the center section, as shown in the partial quilt assembly. Repeat on opposite side. Repeat for remaining sides.
12. Trim quilt if needed to 25" x 25".
13. Appliqué a G heart to each F patch, referring to partial quilt assembly for placement.

Assembling the Quilt Top

1. Sew the gold borders to the sides of the quilt. Sew a blue J patch to each end of the remaining gold borders. Sew the borders to the top and bottom. Press the seam allowances toward the borders.
2. Embroider or fuse a star shape on each J patch, if desired.
3. Sew the narrow white borders to the sides of the quilt. Sew the narrow white borders to the top and bottom.
4. To strip piece the checkerboard borders, sew the flag print and the white solid into strips $1\frac{1}{2}$" wide by the width of the leftover fabric. Join the strips into band 1 and band 2. Press seam allowances toward the dark fabric. Cut each type of band into sixty $1\frac{1}{2}$"-wide segments.

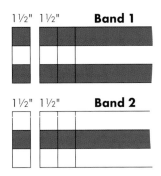

5. Join twenty-seven segments to make each side border, alternating band types and referring to

the quilt assembly for color placement. Sew the borders to the sides of the quilt.

Quilt Assembly

6. Join thirty-three segments to make the top border and thirty-three segments to make the bottom border, alternating band types. Sew the borders to the top and bottom of the quilt.

7. Sew 1½"-wide white borders to the sides of the quilt. Sew 1½"-wide white borders to the top and bottom. Press the seam allowances toward the checkerboard borders.

Quilting and Finishing

1. Layer and baste the quilt backing, batting, and top.

2. Quilt in-the-ditch around the compass points, adding an extra quilted point in each tan patch in the small compasses. Quilt concentric circles around the center compass. Echo quilt ¾" apart around the hearts and small compass circles. Quilt diagonal lines through the small checkerboard border patches and extend the quilting into the outer white border.

3. Trim quilt backing and batting even with the quilt top.

4. Join 2¼"-wide strips end to end to make the binding. Bind the quilt.

Quilting Placement

Rotary Cutting
Measurements include ¼" seam allowance. Align arrows with lengthwise or crosswise grain of fabric.

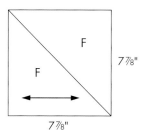

7⅞"

7⅞"

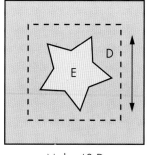

Make 48 D
Make 4 E & 16 reduced E

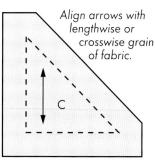

Align arrows with lengthwise or crosswise grain of fabric.

Make 48

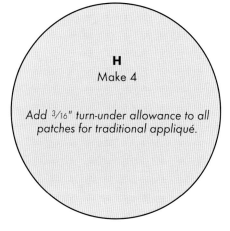

H
Make 4

Add ³⁄₁₆" turn-under allowance to all patches for traditional appliqué.

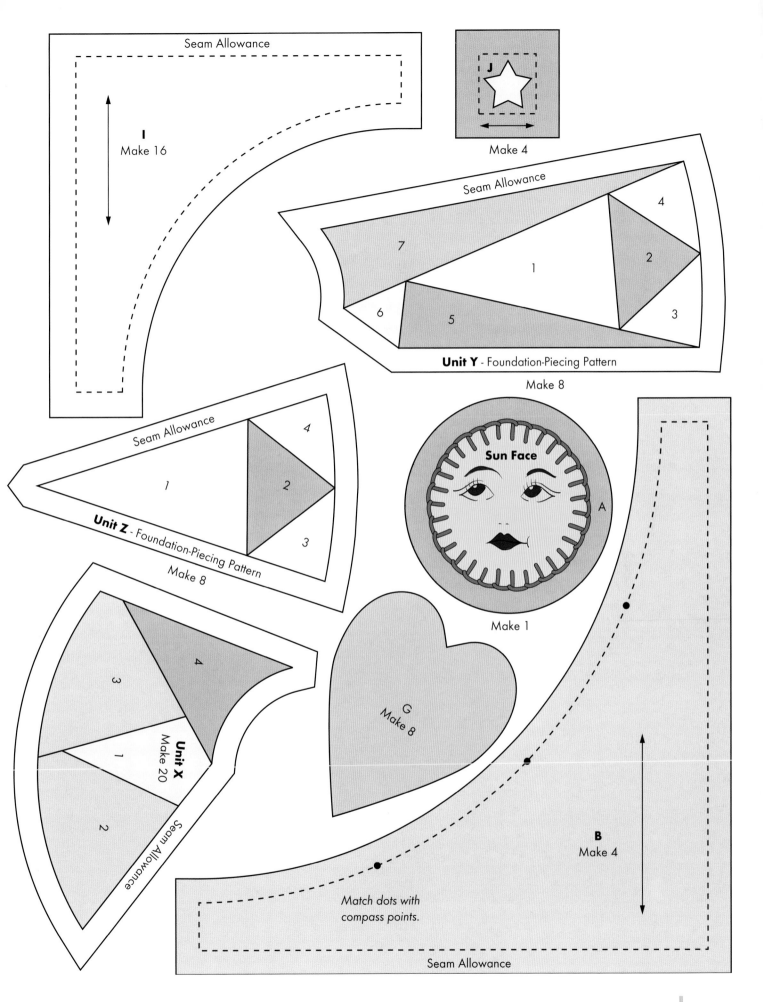

I
Make 16

Seam Allowance

J
Make 4

Seam Allowance

7

4

1

2

3

6

5

Unit Y - Foundation-Piecing Pattern
Make 8

Seam Allowance

4

1

2

3

Unit Z - Foundation-Piecing Pattern
Make 8

Sun Face

A

Make 1

3

4

1

2

Unit X
Make 20

Seam Allowance

G
Make 8

B
Make 4

Match dots with
compass points.

Seam Allowance

Zigzag Path

by Susan Dague

INTERMEDIATE ◆◆

Susan Dague of Piedmont, California, designed *Zigzag Path* after taking a class to learn to use prints, plaids, and stripes more effectively. She challenged herself to find a traditional block that would present stripes in an interesting manner and found what she was looking for in the Quartered Star block, with the blocks set side by side.

Designed and made by Susan Dague.

MATERIALS AND CUTTING

Block Size:	9" x 9"	
Quilt Size:	61½" x 61½"	

Requirements are based on 42" fabric width.

Borders include 2" extra length plus seam allowances.

Read all instructions before cutting. Cut foundation-piecing patches ¾" larger than pattern.

Materials	Yards	Cutting
Gold Stripe	1⅛	
foundation-piecing		12 strips 3" x 42" for #1 and 2 patches
Tan Print	⅜	
inner borders (sides)		2 at 1¾" x 47½"
inner borders (top/bottom)		2 at 1¾" x 50"
Dark Purple	⅜	
middle borders (sides)		2 at 1½" x 50"
middle borders (top/bottom)		2 at 1½" x 52"
Purple Check	1⅞	
outer borders (sides)		2 at 6½" x 52"
outer borders (top/bottom)		2 at 6½" x 64"
binding		7 strips 2¼" x 42"
Large Plaid	⅜	25 A 3½" x 3½" patches
Purple and Blue Scraps	1⅛	
foundation-piecing		12 strips 3" x 42" for #1 and 2 patches
Medium Print Scraps	¾	
foundation-piecing		8 strips 3" x 42" for #2 patches
Backing	3¾	2 panels 33" x 65"
Batting		65" x 65"

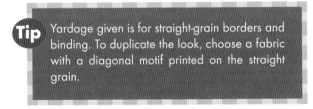

Tip Yardage given is for straight-grain borders and binding. To duplicate the look, choose a fabric with a diagonal motif printed on the straight grain.

Getting Started

Wash and press fabrics. Cut the patches and other pieces as listed in the materials and cutting box. Refer to page 92 for Quilting Basics.

Making the Blocks

1. Trace or photocopy 100 of the foundation-piecing pattern.
2. Foundation-piece the fabric units in numerical order, following the arrows on the pattern to align the grain of the fabrics and referring to photo and block piecing for fabric placement.
3. Referring to the block piecing, sew a fabric unit to one edge of an A patch, sewing a partial seam, as indicated by the *. Moving in a counterclockwise direction, sew a second fabric unit to the A patch, sewing a complete seam. Continue in a counterclockwise direction, sewing four fabric units to the A patch. Complete the first seam.

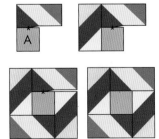

Block Piecing
Make 25

Assembling the Quilt Top

1. Join the blocks in five rows of five blocks each, referring to photo for placement.
2. Join the rows.
3. Sew the inner borders to the sides of the quilt and trim. Sew the inner borders to the top and bottom and trim.
4. Sew the center borders to the sides of the quilt and trim. Sew the center borders to the top and bottom and trim.
5. Sew the outer borders to the sides of the quilt and trim. Sew the outer borders to the top and bottom and trim. Press the seam allowances toward the borders.
6. Remove the paper.

Quilting and Finishing

1. Mark single and double quilting lines as shown in quilting placement, following the zigzag design of the quilt. Mark quilting lines in the tan border, crossing over into the triangles of the quilt. Beginning in the center of each border, mark fourteen double diamond quilting motifs in each outer border, matching the dots. Mark 2" and 2½" squares on point in each corner.

Quilting Placement

2. Layer and baste the quilt backing, batting, and top.
3. Quilt the lines and motifs as marked.
4. Trim quilt backing and batting even with the quilt top.
5. Join 2¼"-wide strips diagonally to make the binding. Bind the quilt.

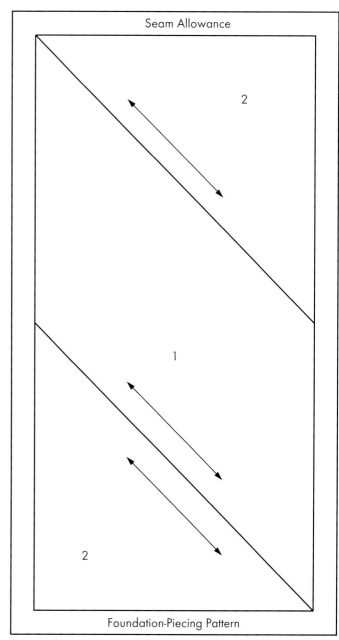

Foundation-Piecing Pattern

Pattern is the reverse of the finished block.
Align arrows with lengthwise or crosswise grain of fabric.

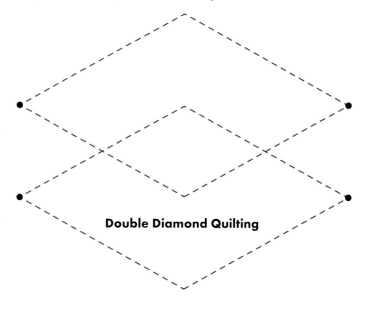

Double Diamond Quilting

Fine Feathered Flock

by Julia Livingston

INTERMEDIATE ◆◇

One way to piece a chicken, by cutting individual patches from templates, has been around since long before 1928, when this block first appeared in *Needlecraft Magazine*. To create this flock, paper-foundation piecing seems the perfect way to simplify the construction and update the classic chicken block. Quiltmakers who have some experience with paper-foundation piecing will have no trouble making this flock come alive. What's more, a change in fabric selections will easily transform these winged barnyard creatures into a quilt-top gathering of gobblers for a Thanksgiving-inspired design.

Designed and made by Julia Livingston.

Block Size: 6" x 6"

Quilt Size: 29" x 42½"

Requirements are based on 42" fabric width.

Borders are the exact length required plus seam allowances.

Read all instructions before cutting. Cut foundation-piecing patches ¾" larger than pattern.

Materials	Yards	Cutting
White Print	⅛	2 chickens
White/Black Print	1⅛	chicken block backgrounds
Gold Print	1	3 chickens; 74 C, 4 D patches;
		beaks and feet as desired
Red Print	¾	5 chickens; 24 B patches
binding		4 strips 2¼" x 42"
Black Print	1⅜	5 chickens; 74 C, 4 D patches
sashing		38 A patches 1¼" x 6½"
Yellow Scraps		beaks and feet as desired
Backing	1⅜	1 panel 33" x 47"
Batting		33" x 47"

Tip For best use of fabric, cut a strip 1½" wide from each chicken fabric and the white/black background print for piecing the small triangles.

Getting Started

Wash and press fabrics. Cut the patches and other pieces as listed in the materials and cutting box. Refer to page 92 for Quilting Basics.

Making the Blocks

1. Trace or photocopy fifteen of the foundation-piecing pattern.
2. Foundation-piece the fabric units in numerical order. All the chicken blocks are sewn in eight sections and then joined.

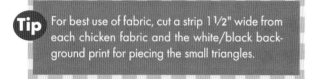

Chicken Block Piecing
Make 15

Assembling the Quilt Top

1. Join sashing and chicken blocks to make a horizontal row, referring to quilt photo for color placement and partial quilt assembly.

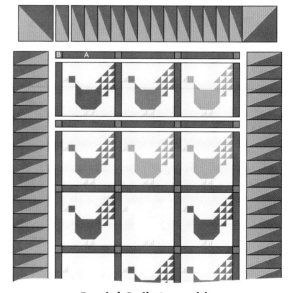

Partial Quilt Assembly

2. Make five rows.

3. Join sashing and B patches to make a horizontal sash row, referring to partial quilt assembly.

4. Make six rows.

5. Join sash rows and chicken-block rows, alternating rows and referring to quilt photo and partial quilt assembly for placement.

6. Remove the paper.

7. Press the seam allowances toward the sashing.

8. Sew a gold D patch to a black D patch to make a corner unit.

Corner Unit
Make 4

9. Sew a gold C patch to a black C patch to make a border unit.

Border Unit
Make 74

10. Join twenty-three border units to make a side border. Make two side borders.

11. Join fourteen border units to make the top border. Sew a corner unit to each end. Repeat for the bottom border.

12. Sew the side borders to the sides of the quilt and trim. Sew the top and bottom borders to the top and bottom and trim. Press the seam allowances toward the borders.

Quilting and Finishing

1. Mark diagonal quilting lines in the blocks and sashing.

2. Layer and baste the quilt backing, batting, and top.

3. Quilt the marked lines and in-the-ditch around the patches in the border.

4. Trim quilt backing and batting even with the quilt top.

5. Join 2¼"-wide strips diagonally to make the binding. Bind the quilt.

Rotary Cutting
Measurements include
¼" seam allowance.
Align arrows with lengthwise
or crosswise grain of fabric.

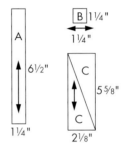

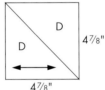

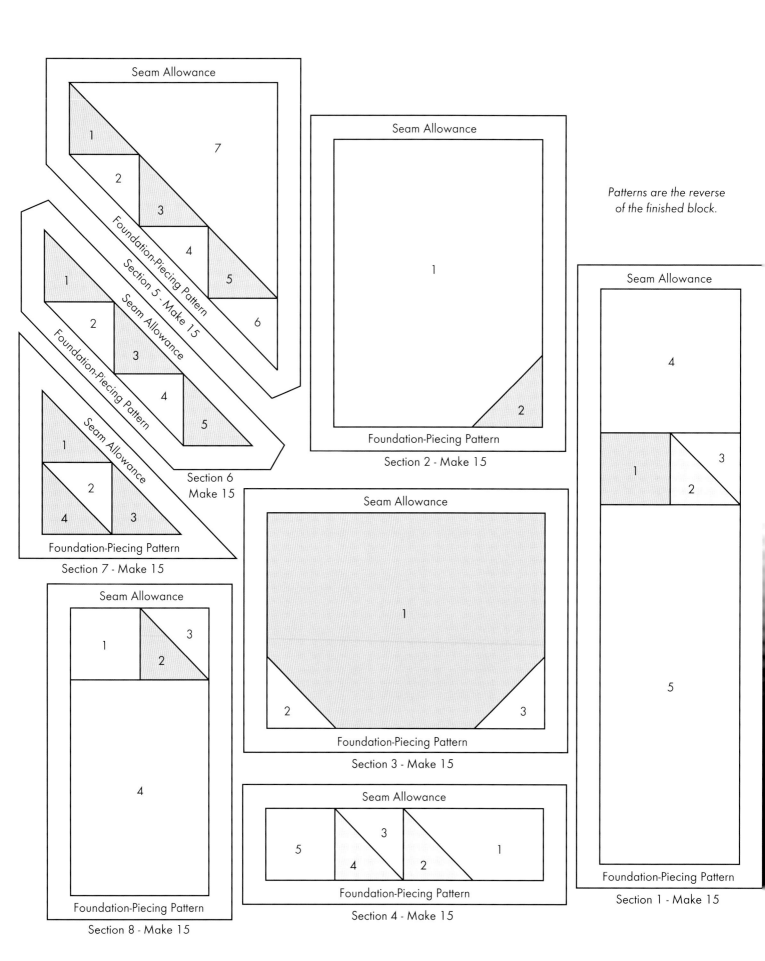

Seam Allowance

1

2

3

4

5

6

7

Foundation-Piecing Pattern
Section 5 - Make 15

Seam Allowance

1

2

3

4

5

6

Section 6
Make 15

Seam Allowance

1

2

3

4

Foundation-Piecing Pattern
Section 7 - Make 15

Seam Allowance

1

2

Foundation-Piecing Pattern
Section 2 - Make 15

*Patterns are the reverse
of the finished block.*

Seam Allowance

4

1

2

3

5

Foundation-Piecing Pattern
Section 1 - Make 15

Seam Allowance

1

2

3

Foundation-Piecing Pattern
Section 3 - Make 15

Seam Allowance

1

2

3

4

Foundation-Piecing Pattern
Section 8 - Make 15

Seam Allowance

5

4

3

2

1

Foundation-Piecing Pattern
Section 4 - Make 15

Delectable Stars

by Brenda Henning

INTERMEDIATE ◆◇

Today's quiltmakers often find design ideas by looking at old patterns in a new way. Such was the case with *Delectable Stars*. The designer combined two traditional patterns, Nancy Page's Ribbon Quilt and the pieced unit from Delectable Mountains. The flexibility of the Delectable Mountains unit gave the designer ideas about several additional ways to set the units. Her ideas are included on the following pages. After seeing the designer's version of this quilt at a show, Marilyn Badger made a pink-and-purple version, shown on page 63.

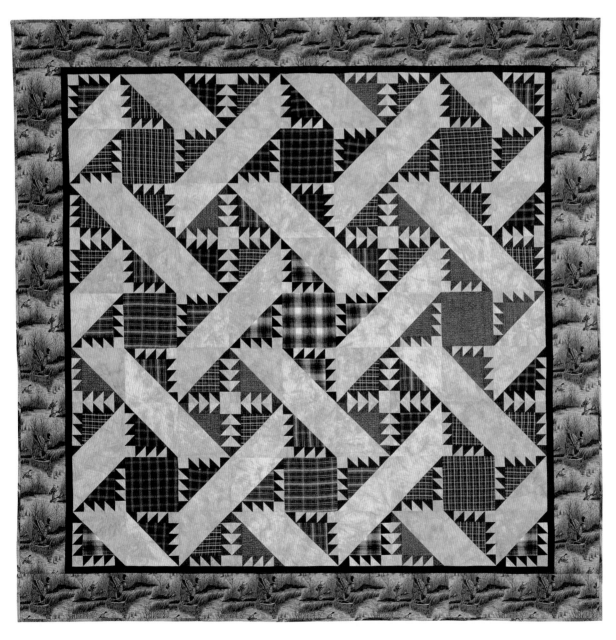

Designed and made by Brenda Henning.

Unit Size:	7½"
Block Size:	22½" x 22½"
Quilt Size:	83½" x 83½"

Requirements are based on 42" fabric width.

Borders include 2" extra length plus seam allowances.

Read all instructions before cutting. Cut foundation-piecing patches ¾" larger than pattern.

Materials	Yards	Cutting
Tan Solid [Gray/Blue]	4⅛	72 B patches
foundation-piecing		72 each #1, 3, 5, 7 patches for star unit 1
		72 each #2, 4, 6 patches for star unit 2
Red Print	2⅛ [½]	
inner borders (sides)		2 at 1½" x 70"
inner borders (top/bottom)		2 at 1½" x 72"
Tan/Red Print	3⅛ [2]	
outer borders (sides)		2 at 7½" x 72"
outer borders (top/bottom)		2 at 7½" x 86"
binding		9 strips 2¼" x 42"
Brown/Red Solid [Pink/Purple]	2¼	
foundation-piecing		72 each #2, 4, 6, 8 patches for star unit 1
		72 each #1, 3, 5, 7 patches for star unit 2
Brown/Red Plaid [Pink/Purple]	1¾	9 A, 72 C patches
Backing	7½	3 panels 30" x 88"
Batting		88" x 88"

Colors given in [ ] are for the pink-and-purple version of this quilt.

Yardage given in [ ] is for borders cut crosswise and pieced. If making the borders in this manner, add ¾ yard of the same fabric for binding.

Tip Yardage is given for both quilts in the materials and cutting box. However, there are a few differences in fabric placement. The wide, outer borders in the tan quilt are made using a large-scale print, while the outer borders of the pink-and-purple version are made using the same gray/blue fabric used in the block background patches. The small triangles in the tan quilt are made using solid fabrics, and the larger triangles (C patches) are made using plaids. In the pink quilt, the same fabric is used for those patches within each of the units.

Getting Started

Wash and press fabrics. Cut the patches and other pieces as listed in the materials and cutting box. Refer to page 92 for Quilting Basics.

Making the Blocks

1. Trace or photocopy seventy-two of star unit 1 and seventy-two of star unit 2.
2. Foundation-piece the units in numerical order.
3. Join a star unit 1 and a star unit 2 with a C patch to make a delectable star unit.

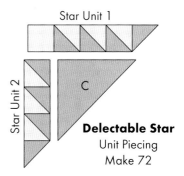

Delectable Star
Unit Piecing
Make 72

4. Make seventy-two delectable star units.

5. Join eight delectable star units with eight B patches and one A patch to make a block, being careful to turn the units as shown in the block piecing so that the design will not be interrupted.

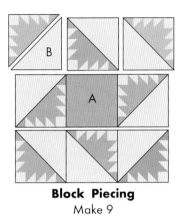

Block Piecing
Make 9

Assembling the Quilt Top

1. Join the blocks in three rows of three blocks each.
2. Join the rows.
3. Sew the inner borders to the sides of the quilt and trim. Sew the inner borders to the top and bottom and trim.
4. Sew the outer borders to the sides of the quilt and trim. Sew the outer borders to the top and bottom and trim.
5. Remove the paper.

Quilting and Finishing

1. Layer and baste the quilt backing, batting, and top.
2. Quilt in-the-ditch around the smallest patches. Quilt graceful curves in the B patches. Quilt along the printed motifs in the outer border. For the pink-and-purple version, quilt in-the-ditch around the smallest patches. Machine quilt diagonal lines in the B patches, crossing the seams between blocks. Quilt concentric circles in the A patches, half circles in the C patches, and overall stippling in the star unit patches. Quilt continuous leafy loops in the outer border.
3. Trim quilt backing and batting even with the quilt top.

4. Join 2¼"-wide strips diagonally to make the binding. Bind the quilt.

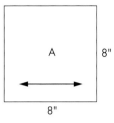

Rotary Cutting
Measurements include ¼" seam allowance. Align arrow with lengthwise or crosswise grain of fabric.

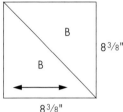

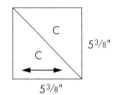

Variations

The delectable star units can be arranged in a variety of designs, such as the four variations shown on the following page. The number of units, A patches, and B patches needed for each variation are included under the variation. Quiltmakers with an adventurous spirit may wish to experiment further with unit placement before sewing the units together.

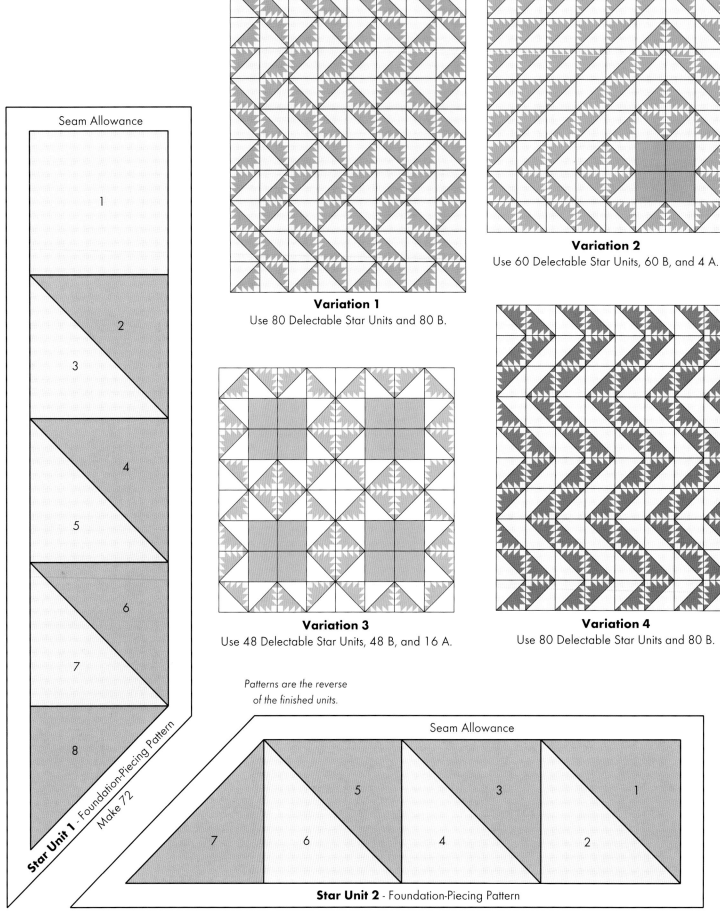

Seam Allowance

1

2

3

4

5

6

7

8

Star Unit 1 - Foundation-Piecing Pattern

Make 72

Variation 1
Use 80 Delectable Star Units and 80 B.

Variation 2
Use 60 Delectable Star Units, 60 B, and 4 A.

Variation 3
Use 48 Delectable Star Units, 48 B, and 16 A.

Variation 4
Use 80 Delectable Star Units and 80 B.

*Patterns are the reverse
of the finished units.*

Seam Allowance

5

7

6

3

4

1

2

Star Unit 2 - Foundation-Piecing Pattern

Make 72

Promises

by Tone Haugen-Cogburn

Double Wedding Ring quilts and other circular patterns have long fascinated designer Tone Haugen-Cogburn. *Promises* was her first attempt to design an original block. After piecing the blocks together, a secondary pattern evolved. The designer thought the large, dark circles looked empty, so she designed five appliqué motifs to fill some of them.

Designed and made by Tone Haugen-Cogburn.

Block Size:		11½" x 11½"
Quilt Size:		54" x 54"

Requirements are based on 42" fabric width.

Borders include extra length for mitering.

Read all instructions before cutting. Cut foundation-piecing patches ¾" larger than pattern.

Materials	Yards	Cutting
Black Print	2⅞	56 A, 92 B, 8 C, 4 D patches
borders		4 at 3½" x 65½"
Green Print	1	8 A patches
binding		6 strips 2¼" x 42"
folded border		6 strips 1" x 35"
Blue Scraps	⅞	
foundation-piecing		64 each #1, 2, 3 patches for diamond section 1
Gold/Yellow Scraps	1½	96 B patches; leaves and berries
foundation-piecing		64 #4 patches for diamond section 1;
		64 each #1, 2 patches for diamond section 2
Green Scraps		leaves
Backing	3⅜	2 panels 30" x 58"
Batting		58" x 58"

Supplies: Green embroidery floss

Getting Started

Wash and press fabrics. Cut the patches and other pieces as listed in the materials and cutting box. Refer to page 92 for Quilting Basics.

Making the Blocks

1. Trace or photocopy sixty-four A patches, sixty-four diamond section 1, and sixty-four diamond section 2.
2. Foundation-piece the diamond sections in numerical order.
3. Join a diamond section 1 with a diamond section 2 along their curved edges, matching the dots, to make a diamond unit.
4. Make sixty-four diamond units.

5. Join four diamond units along their short, straight edges, referring to block piecing.

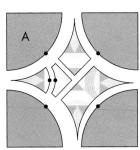

Block Piecing
Make 16

6. Join four diamond units with four A patches to make a block, matching the dots on the A patches with the unit seams and placing the green A patches randomly in eight of the blocks.

Assembling the Quilt Top

1. Make four rows of four blocks each.
2. Join the rows.
3. Remove the paper.
4. Prepare the appliqué leaf and berry patches.

5. Arrange the appliqué patches on the circles, referring to appliqué motifs. (Intersecting lines indicate where the A patches join.) If desired, make full-size patterns for motif positioning. To make full-size patterns, enlarge the appliqué motifs 400% on a photocopy machine.

   Note: Appliqué pattern enlargement may need to be done in two steps of 200% each.

6. Appliqué the patches.

7. Embroider the motif stems using the Outline stitch.

Outline Stitch

8. Join twenty-three black B patches side by side with twenty-four gold/yellow B patches, alternating patch colors, to make a border. Sew a C patch to each end.

9. Make four borders.

10. Sew borders to the top and bottom of the quilt. Sew a D patch to each end of the remaining borders. Sew the borders to the sides.

11. Join green border strips to make four 50"-long borders.

12. Fold the green border strips in half lengthwise, right sides out, and press. Align a green border strip with one edge of the quilt, placing strip on the right side of the quilt and keeping raw edges even. Baste or pin in place. Trim the ends even with the quilt's raw edge. Repeat for the opposite side. Repeat for the remaining sides, overlapping the strips at the corners. Do not press.

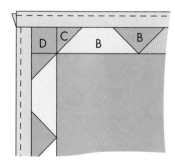

13. Sew the black borders to the quilt. The folded green strips will be caught in the seams.

14. Press the black border strips away from the quilt center. Press the folded green strips toward the quilt center so that the green strips cover the points of the gold triangles.

15. Miter the corners of the black borders, referring to Quilting Basics on page 92.

Quilting and Finishing

1. Layer and baste the quilt backing, batting, and top.

2. Quilt in-the-ditch around the appliqué motifs. Quilt a 1" grid around the appliqué in the A patches. Repeat the grid in the A patches that have no appliqué.

3. Trim quilt backing and batting even with the quilt top.

4. Join 2¼"-wide strips diagonally to make the binding. Bind the quilt.

Rotary Cutting

Measurements include
¼" seam allowance.
Align arrows with lengthwise
or crosswise grain of fabric.

B B B B 3¼"
B
3¼"

C C 1⅞"
1⅞"

D 1½"
1½"

Appliqué Berries

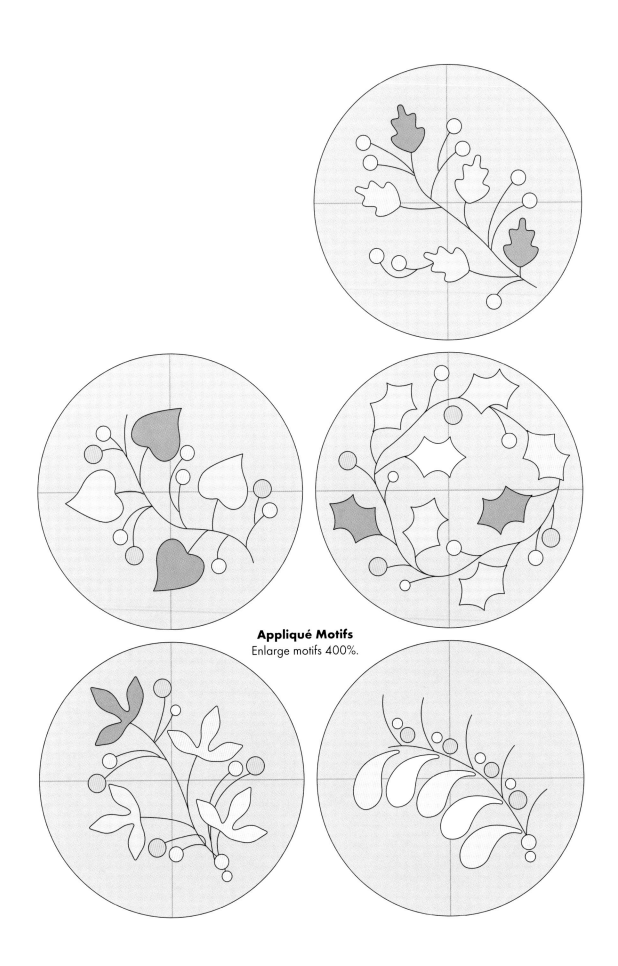

Appliqué Motifs
Enlarge motifs 400%.

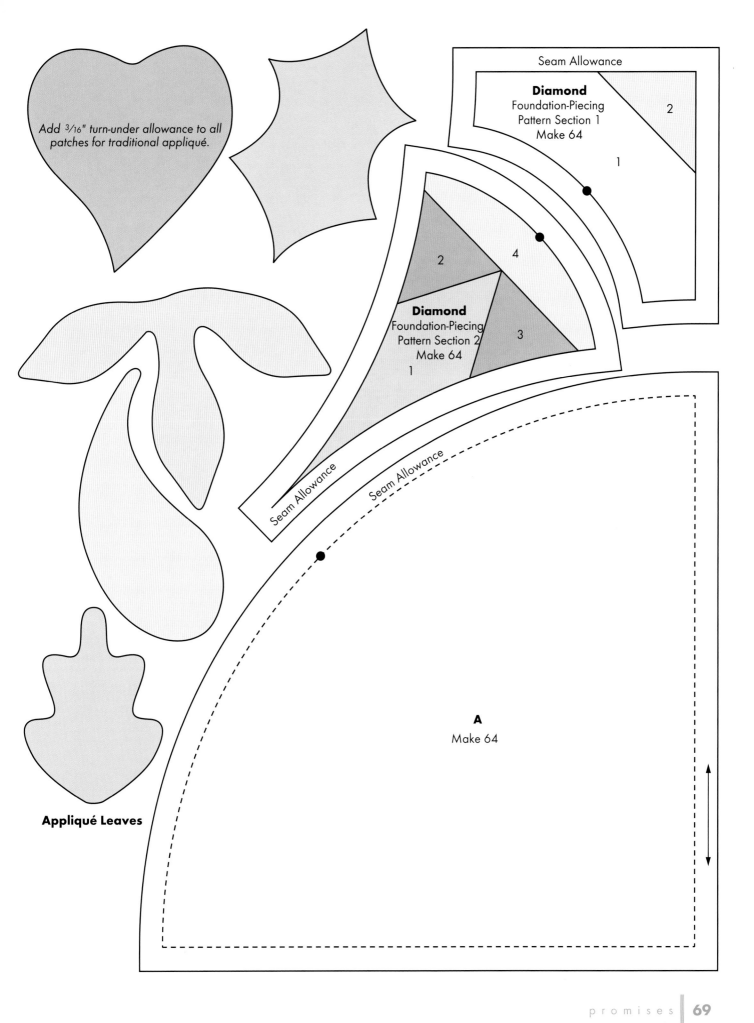

Add 3/16" turn-under allowance to all patches for traditional appliqué.

Diamond
Foundation-Piecing
Pattern Section 1
Make 64

Seam Allowance

2

1

2

4

Diamond
Foundation-Piecing
Pattern Section 2
Make 64

2

3

1

Seam Allowance

Seam Allowance

Appliqué Leaves

A
Make 64

Basket Bouquets

by *Quiltmaker* staff

CHALLENGING ◆◆◆

This quilt would make a great group project! There's something here for everyone! Those whose passion is piecing could work on the foundation piecing, while appliqué fans could fill the baskets with flowers, and those new to the technique could add just a few patches. Give each blockmaker a 5" x 17" piece of the background fabric and enough strips for the baskets. Be sure each block-maker signs his or her name in patch 6, which provides an ideal spot for signing.

Designed by the *Quiltmaker* staff. Made by Lucy Brown.

MATERIALS AND CUTTING

Block Size:		7½" x 7½"
Quilt Size:		30½" x 30½"

Requirements are based on 42" fabric width.

Borders are the exact length required plus seam allowances.

Read all instructions before cutting. Cut foundation-piecing patches ¾" larger than pattern.

Materials	Yards	Cutting
Assorted Scraps		appliqué patches C–L and bias stems
Floral Print Scraps		
foundation-piecing		4 #1 patches
Pink Print	⅛	16 A patches
Cream Print	⅝	
foundation-piecing		5 #1 patches; 9 each #13, 14, 15, 16 patches
Tan Print	½	24 B patches
Light Gold Print	¼	
foundation-piecing		9 #6 patches
Medium Gold Print	¼	
foundation-piecing		9 each #5, 7, 9 patches
Dark Gold Print	½	
foundation-piecing		9 each #2, 3, 11, 12 patches
Medium Brown Print Scraps		
foundation-piecing		9 #8 patches
Dark Brown Print	¼	
foundation-piecing		9 each #4, 10 patches
Multicolor Print	⅜	
binding		4 strips 2¼" x 42"
Backing	1⅜	
backing		1 panel 35" x 35"
sleeve		9" x 30½"
Batting		35" x 35"

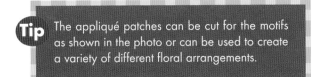

Tip The appliqué patches can be cut for the motifs as shown in the photo or can be used to create a variety of different floral arrangements.

Getting Started

Wash and press fabrics. Cut the patches and other pieces as listed in the materials and cutting box. Refer to page 92 for Quilting Basics.

Making the Blocks

1. Trace or photocopy nine of the foundation-piecing pattern.
2. Foundation-piece the fabric units in numerical order.

3. Add one A patch and two B patches to each foundation-pieced basket, making the patches part of the basket block. By making the A and B patches part of the block, the appliqué patches will be able to spill over into the sashes.

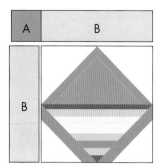

Block Piecing
Make 9

4. Remove the paper.
5. Prepare the appliqué patches.
6. Arrange the appliqué patches on the blocks as desired, referring to photo for placement.
7. Appliqué the patches.

Assembling the Quilt Top

1. Sew one A patch and one B patch together to make a side border.

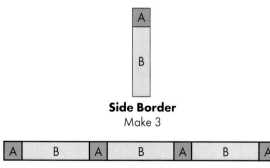

Side Border
Make 3

Bottom Border Make 1

2. Make three side borders.
3. Make three rows of three blocks each, adding a side border at the end of each row.
4. Join the rows.
5. Sew four A patches and three B patches together to make a bottom border.
6. Sew the bottom border to the bottom of the quilt.

Quilting and Finishing

1. Layer and baste the quilt backing, batting, and top.
2. Quilt in-the-ditch around the A and B patches, and around the #1, 2, 3, 6, 11, and 12 foundation patches.
3. Trim quilt backing and batting even with the quilt top.
4. Join 2¼"-wide strips diagonally to make the binding. Bind the quilt.
5. Sew a sleeve to the backing for display purposes.

Rotary Cutting
*Measurements include
¼" seam allowance.
Align arrows with lengthwise
or crosswise grain of fabric.*

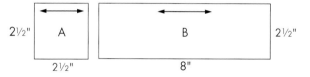

Add 3/16" turn-under allowances to all appliqué patches.

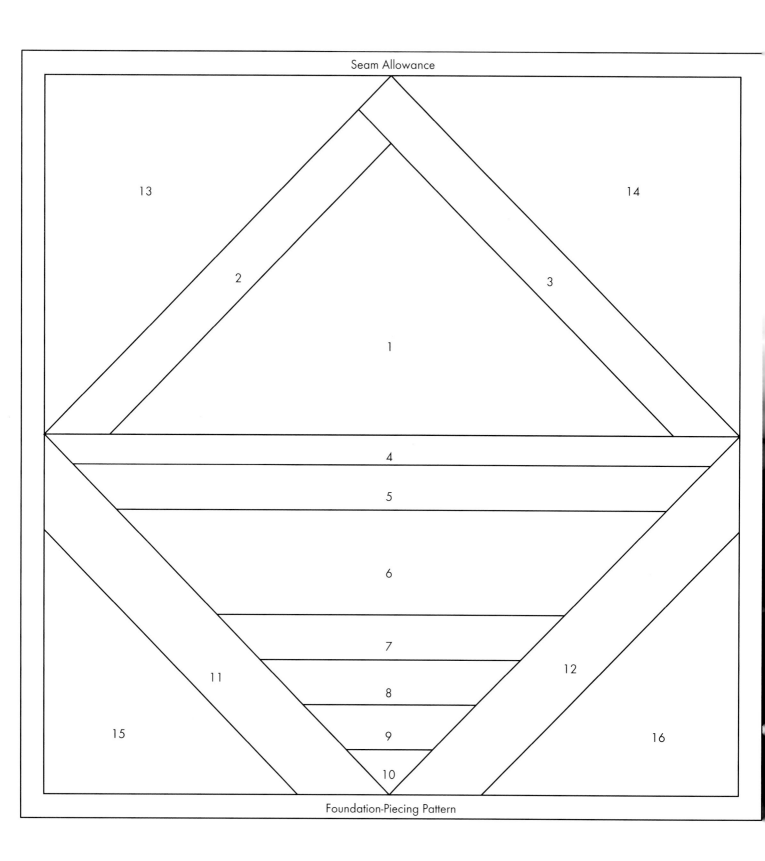

Seam Allowance

13   14

2   3

1

4

5

6

7

11   12

8

15   9   16

10

Foundation-Piecing Pattern

Full Circle

CHALLENGING ◆◆◆

by Tone Haugen-Cogburn

When Tone Haugen-Cogburn saw an antique quilt with a triangular Wedding Ring block, she decided to interpret the design in a contemporary manner. She turned the rings into football shapes that are not pieced and designed a pieced center instead of keeping the traditional solid white patches. *Full Circle* is one of several quilts in which the designer has explored circular shapes.

Designed and made by Tone Haugen-Cogburn.

MATERIALS AND CUTTING

Quilt Size: 35" x 40¼"

Requirements are based on 42" fabric width.

Read all instructions before cutting. Cut foundation-piecing patches ¾" larger than pattern.

Materials	Yards	Cutting
Red Print	1¼	24 A patches
Red/Black Print	5/8	4 B, 2 C, 1 D, 1Dr patches
Black/Red Print	1/2	8 A patches
Red Solid	1/2	
bias binding		2¼" x 4¾ yards
Red Scraps	1/2	
foundation-piecing		60 #1 patches
Yellow Scraps	3/8	
foundation-piecing		60 #4 patches
Green Scraps	1/2	
foundation-piecing		60 each #2, 3 patches
Backing	1⅜	1 panel 39" x 44"
Batting		39" x 44"

Getting Started

Wash and press fabrics. Cut the patches and other pieces as listed in the materials and cutting box. Refer to page 92 for Quilting Basics.

Making the Blocks

1. Trace or photocopy sixty of the foundation-piecing pattern.
2. Foundation-piece the fabric units in numerical order.
3. Join three fabric units together along their short, straight edges to make a center unit.

Center Unit Piecing
Make 20

4. Sew three A patches along the curved edges of a center unit, matching the dots and referring to circle block piecing, to make a circle block. Note that the A patches are sewn to one another along part of their edges.

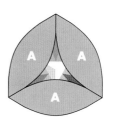

Circle Block Piecing
Make 8

5. Sew two A patches and one B patch along the curved edges of a center unit, matching the dots and referring to bottom block piecing, to make a bottom block. Note that the A and B patches are sewn to one another along part of their edges.

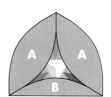

Bottom Block Piecing
Make 2

6. Remove the paper.

Assembling the Quilt Top

1. Join the circle blocks and bottom blocks with the A, B, C, D, and Dr patches, referring to the quilt assembly.

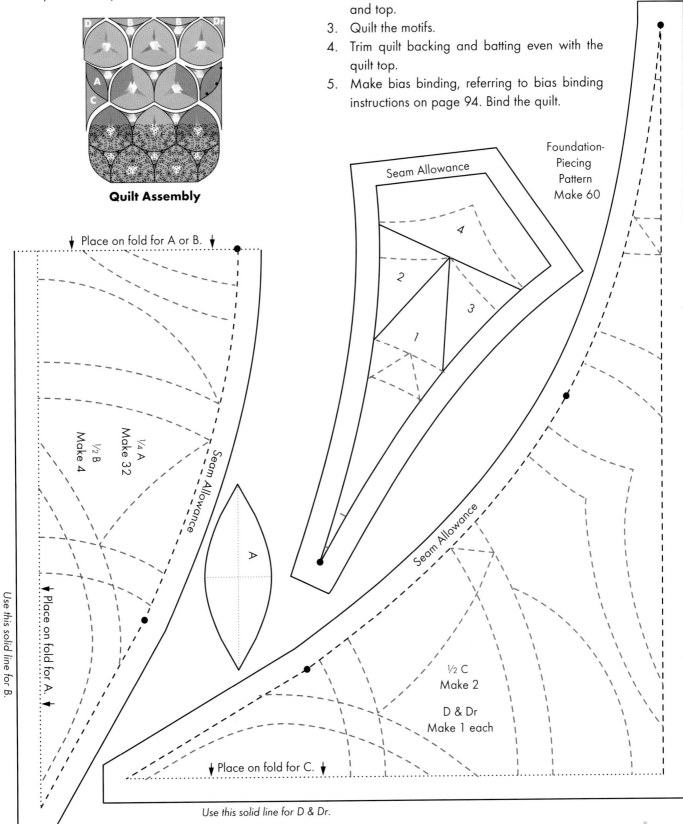

Quilt Assembly

Quilting and Finishing

1. Mark the quilting motifs from the center units and from the A, B, C, and D patches.
2. Layer and baste the quilt backing, batting, and top.
3. Quilt the motifs.
4. Trim quilt backing and batting even with the quilt top.
5. Make bias binding, referring to bias binding instructions on page 94. Bind the quilt.

Place on fold for A or B.

Seam Allowance

Foundation-Piecing Pattern Make 60

4

2

3

1

Seam Allowance

¼ A
Make 32

½ B
Make 4

A

Seam Allowance

½ C
Make 2

D & Dr
Make 1 each

Use this solid line for B.

Place on fold for A.

↓ Place on fold for C. ↓

Use this solid line for D & Dr.

Sparkling Candles

CHALLENGING ◆◆◆

by Mary Leman Austin

One of the most-beloved holidays in the Jewish religion is Hanukkah, the Festival of Lights. During this eight-day celebration, the Menorah, or candelabrum, is lit each night, with the number of candles increasing nightly until all eight are lit. The central candle is used to light the others. In this quilt, the eight blocks show the progression of the candle lighting. Pressed for time? One framed block will make a lovely wall hanging.

Designed and made by Mary Leman Austin.

Getting Started

Wash and press fabrics. Cut the patches and other pieces as listed in the materials and cutting box. Refer to page 92 for Quilting Basics.

Making the Blocks

1. Trace or photocopy eight unit 1, sixty-four unit 2, and eight unit 3.
2. Foundation-piece the fabric units in numerical order.

MATERIALS AND CUTTING

Block Size:		9½" x 16½"
Quilt Size:		38" x 33½"

Requirements are based on 42" fabric width.

Borders include extra length for mitering.

Read all instructions before cutting. Cut foundation-piecing patches ¾" larger than pattern.

Materials	Yards	Cutting
Red Solid	3/8	candles
Wine Print	1	8 A patches
borders (sides)		2 at 3" x 38½"
borders (top/bottom)		2 at 3" x 43"
binding		4 strips 2¼" x 42"
Silver Print	3/4	candle background
Pink/Gold Print	3/4	*2 C, 4 D, 2 E, 2 Er patches
Pink Print	5/8	8 B patches
Solid Scraps		
Dark Blue		flame background
Yellow		flames
Backing	1 1/8	1 panel 37" x 42"
Batting		37" x 42"

* Refer to Cutting for Directional Fabric before cutting patches C, D, E, and Er.

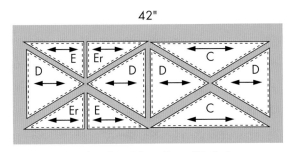

42"

Cutting for Directional Fabric

3. Join the units to make eight candle arcs, referring to Menorah block piecing.

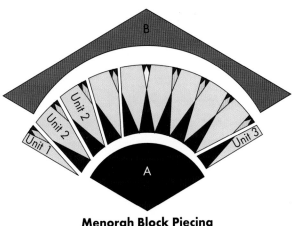

Menorah Block Piecing
Make 8

4. Trace complete A and B patch patterns onto the paper side of freezer paper. Cut out the paper pattern, which does not include seam allowances. Press the freezer-paper patterns to the back side of the fabric and cut out the fabric patches, including ¼" seam allowances. Press the seam allowance along the curved edges of the A and B patches to the back side of the fabric, using the freezer-paper edge to obtain a smooth curve. Make eight A patches and eight B patches.

5. Position the curved edges of the A and B patches along the curved edges of the pieced candle arcs and blindstitch the curves in place. Join one A patch and one B patch to one assembled arc, referring to Menorah block piecing.

6. Remove the paper.

Assembling the Quilt Top

1. Join the Menorah blocks in diagonal rows with C, D, E, and Er patches, referring to partial quilt assembly.
2. Join the rows.

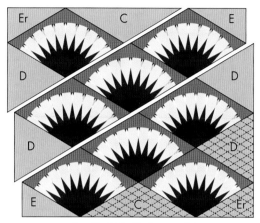

Partial Quilt Assembly

3. Sew the borders to the sides of the quilt. Sew the borders to the top and bottom, mitering the corners. Press the seam allowances toward the borders.

Quilting and Finishing

1. Layer and baste the quilt backing, batting, and top.
2. Quilt in-the-ditch around the smallest patches. Quilt a grid of lines parallel to the edges of the blocks in the C, D, E, and Er patches, referring to quilting lines indicated in the partial quilt assembly.
3. Trim quilt backing and batting even with the quilt top.
4. Join 2¼"-wide strips diagonally to make the binding. Bind the quilt.

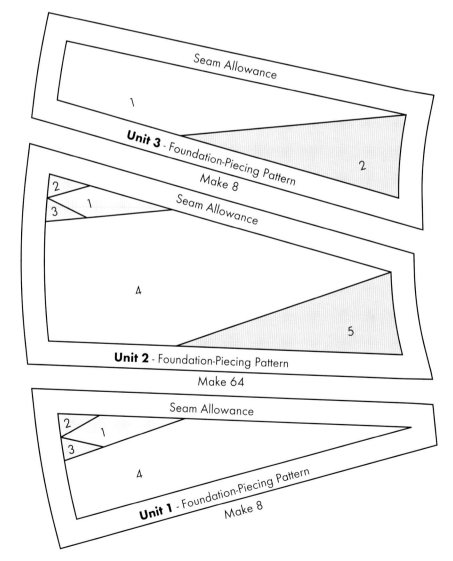

Seam Allowance

1

2

Unit 3 - Foundation-Piecing Pattern

Make 8

2
3
1
Seam Allowance

4

5

Unit 2 - Foundation-Piecing Pattern

Make 64

Seam Allowance

2
3
1

4

Unit 1 - Foundation-Piecing Pattern

Make 8

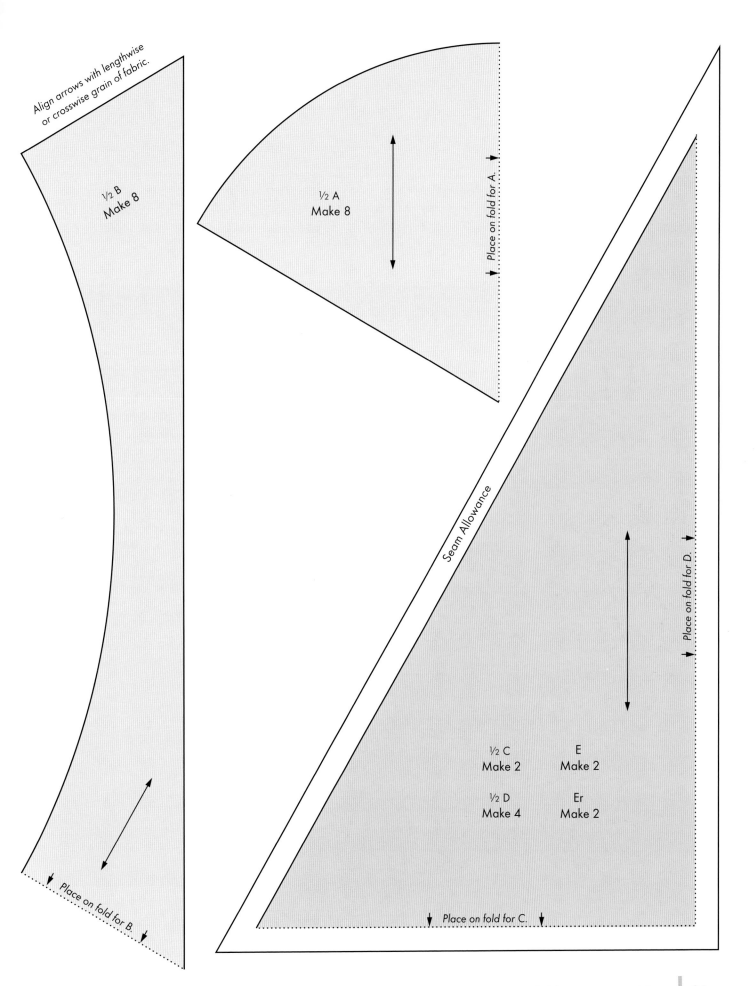

Align arrows with lengthwise or crosswise grain of fabric.

½ B
Make 8

½ A
Make 8

Place on fold for A.

Seam Allowance

Place on fold for D.

½ C
Make 2

E
Make 2

½ D
Make 4

Er
Make 2

Place on fold for B.

Place on fold for C.

Busting Out

CHALLENGING ◆◆◆

by Allison Cooke Brown

This joyous and colorful 57"-square quilt was a finalist in the Quilts: Celebrating the Tradition contest, sponsored by QNM at Quilt Expo IV in Karlsruhe, Germany, in 1994. *Busting Out* is the sixth quilt of a Log-Cabin block series called Sunshine and Shadows, which parallels the designer's five-year recovery from breast cancer.

Designed and made by Allison Cooke Brown.

MATERIALS AND CUTTING

Block Size:		7½" x 7½"
Quilt Size:		57" x 57"

Requirements are based on 42" fabric width.

Borders include extra length for mitering.

Read all instructions before cutting. Cut foundation-piecing patches ¾" larger than pattern.

Materials	Yards	Cutting
Black Solid	2¾	
outer borders		4 at 1¾" x 65"
		104 A, 4 B, 4 Br, 100 #7 patches
Black Print	¼	25 #1 patches
White-and-Black Print	1	
inner borders		4 at 2" x 55"
sashing		40 strips 2" x 8"
Pink Stripe	¼	
center borders		4 at 1" x 54"
Purple Solid	5⁄8	
binding		7 strips 2¼" x 42"
Bright Scraps	4	108 A, 100 each #2, 3, 4, 5, 6 patches
Blue Print	⅛	
setting squares		16 at 2" x 2"
Backing	35⁄8	2 panels 31" x 61"
Batting		61" x 61"

Getting Started

Wash and press fabrics. Cut the patches and other pieces as listed in the materials and cutting box. Refer to page 92 for Quilting Basics.

Making the Blocks

1. Trace or photocopy twenty-five Log Cabin blocks.
2. On the back side of the foundation paper, align the edges of a #1 patch, right side up, with the dashed lines. Pin patch in place to prevent shifting.

3. On the back side of the paper foundation, place a #2 patch on top of the #1 patch, placing right sides of fabric together and keeping raw edges even.

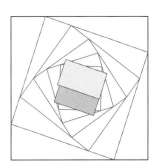

4. Hold the fabric in place and turn the paper over. Re-pin the fabrics from the drawn side and remove the pin (from Step 2) from the fabric side. Sew along the solid line, using short, straight stitches.

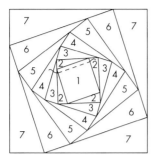

5. Trim the edge of the #2 patch even with the edge of the #1 patch.
6. Press the #2 patch open.

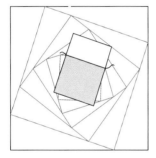

7. Sew the remaining #2 patches around the center.
8. On the back side of the paper foundation, place a #3 patch on top of a #2 patch, placing right sides of fabric together and holding the pattern up to the light to be sure the fabric covers the patch and that there are sufficient seam allowances on all sides.

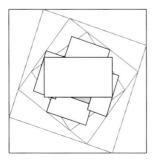

9. Pin patch in place to prevent shifting. Turn the paper over. Re-pin the fabrics from the drawn side and remove the pin from the fabric side. Sew along the solid line, using short, straight stitches.
10. Trim the seam allowance to ¼".
11. Press the #3 patch open.
12. Sew the remaining #3 patches.
13. Continue foundation piecing the fabric units in numerical order, ending with a #7 patch in each corner.
14. Trim the block to 8" x 8".
15. Make twenty-five blocks.

Assembling the Quilt Top

1. Place blocks on a large, flat surface and arrange until satisfied with color placement.
2. Beginning with a block, sew five blocks to four sashing strips, alternating the blocks and sashing, to make one block row. Refer to the partial quilt assembly.

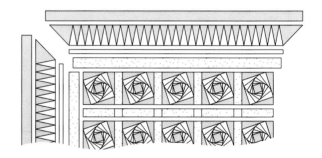

Partial Quilt Assembly

3. Make five block rows.
4. Beginning with a sash, sew five sashing strips to four setting squares, alternating the sashing and setting squares, to make a sash row. Refer to the partial quilt assembly.

5. Make four sash rows.

6. Beginning with a block row, sew five block rows to four sash rows to form the quilt top. Refer to partial quilt assembly.

7. Beginning with a bright scrap A patch, sew twenty-seven bright scrap A patches to twenty-six black A patches, alternating the colors, to make a pieced border. Sew a B patch to the bright A patch at the far left end of the row and a Br patch to the bright A patch at the far right end, being sure to sew the correct side of the B and Br patches to the A patches.

8. Make four pieced borders.

9. Fold a pieced border, an inner border, a center border, and an outer border in half to locate the center of each. Matching the centers, sew the four borders together to make a border unit, referring to the partial quilt assembly.

10. Make four border units.

11. Sew border units to the sides of the quilt. Sew border units to the top and bottom, mitering the corners as if working with a single border piece.

12. Remove the paper.

Quilting and Finishing

1. Layer and baste the quilt backing, batting, and top.

2. Quilt in-the-ditch around the patches and along the border seams.

3. Trim quilt backing and batting even with the quilt top.

4. Join 2¼"-wide strips diagonally to make the binding. Bind the quilt.

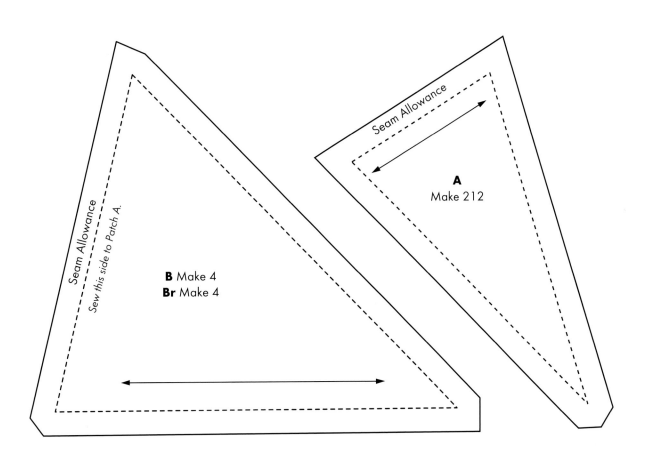

Seam Allowance
Sew this side to Patch A.

B Make 4
Br Make 4

Seam Allowance

A
Make 212

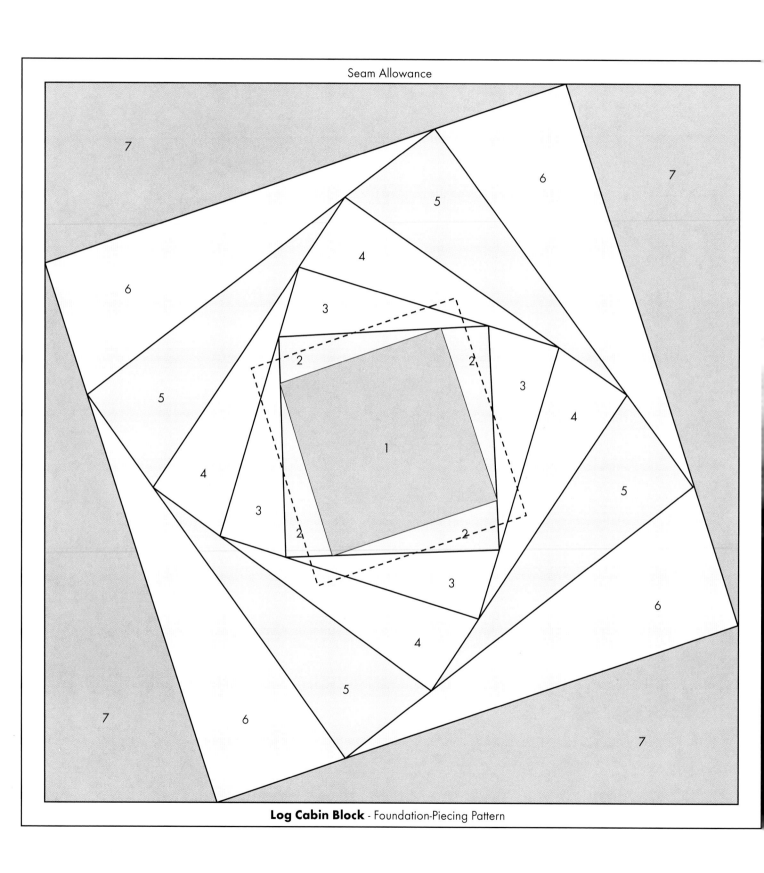

Seam Allowance

Log Cabin Block - Foundation-Piecing Pattern

Wagon Wheels

CHALLENGING ◆◆◆

by Dixie Haywood

The pattern for *Wagon Wheels* was first printed in the *Kansas City Star* in 1934. The designer altered the original so that there would be more small triangles in the blocks, and she made some of the block parts with paper-foundation piecing. In 1934, the *Star* readers didn't have the paper-foundation piecing technique to help them. The quote that ran with the original pattern reads: "For sever-

al weeks this department has been petting the quilt-makers who were beginners by giving them easy patterns. This week the pattern is for experts; none others need try it." Quilters who have experience with paper-foundation piecing, working with curves, and setting in patches will enjoy using this challenging pattern.

Designed and made by Dixie Haywood.

MATERIALS AND CUTTING

Block Size:		16" x 16"
Quilt Size:		76" x 92"

Requirements are based on 42" fabric width.

Borders are the exact length required plus seam allowances.

Read all instructions before cutting. Cut foundation-piecing patches ¾" larger than pattern.

Materials	Yards	Cutting
White Print	1⅞	
foundation-piecing		80 strips 2¼" x 12" for unit 3 #2, 3, 6, 7, 10, 11 patches
Assorted Yellow Scraps	6¼	80 A, 80 B, 120 C patches
foundation-piecing		160 strips 2¼" x 12" for
		unit 1 and unit 2 #2, 3, 6, 7, 10, 11, 14, 15 patches
Light Blue Print	1⅛	40 E patches
Dark Blue Print	1⅛	40 E patches
Blue Print	2⅜	18 G patches 5½" x 16½", 4 H patches 6½" x 6½"
binding		10 strips 2¼" x 42"
Assorted Red Scraps	6	80 D patches
foundation-piecing		240 strips 2¼" x 12" for
		unit 1, unit 2, and unit 3 #1, 4, 5, 8, 9, 12, 13 patches
Red Print	½	18 F patches 1½" x 16½"
Backing	5½	2 panels 40½" x 96"
Batting		80" x 96"

Tip

- Many different red and yellow prints were used to give variety to the designer's quilt. For a more-controlled look, the palette of fabrics can be limited.
- When working with the paper-foundation piecing patterns, make a dot in each triangle that will have red fabric. This will aid in correct placement of the red patches.
- Refer to block piecing for color placement, noting which parts of the units are made from the same red or yellow fabrics. Each 2¼" x 12" fabric strip is long enough to cover the pattern patches of one color in one unit.

Getting Started

Wash and press fabrics. Cut the patches and other pieces as listed in the materials and cutting box. Refer to page 92 for Quilting Basics.

Making the Blocks

1. Trace or photocopy eighty of unit 1, eighty of unit 2, and eighty of unit 3.
2. Foundation-piece the fabric units in numerical order, referring to block piecing for color placement.

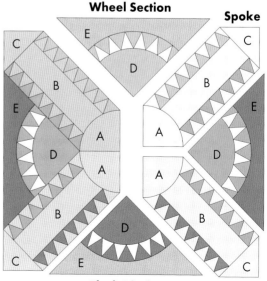

Wheel Section   **Spoke**

Block Piecing
Make 20

3. Sew a D patch, a unit 3, and an E patch together to form a wheel section, referring to block piecing and aligning the dots on the D and E patches with the seams of the triangles. Note the placement of light- and dark-blue E patches in block piecing.

4. Make four wheel sections.

5. Sew an A patch, a unit 1, a unit 2, a B patch, and a C patch together to form a spoke, referring to block piecing and aligning the dots on the A patch with the seams of the triangles.

6. Make four spokes.

7. Join four wheel sections and four spokes to make a block.

8. Press the seam allowances away from the paper-pieced units.

Assembling the Quilt Top

1. Join the blocks in five rows of four blocks each, turning every other block so that the light- and dark-blue E patches alternate as shown in the photo.

2. Join the rows.

3. To make a border unit, sew the long edge of an F patch to the long edge of a G patch.

4. Make dots 2⅞" from the two bottom corners to mark placement location of C patches, as shown in border assembly. Draw a diagonal line between the two dots, using the edge of a ruler to achieve a straight line. Repeat at remaining bottom corner. Cut along the marked lines.

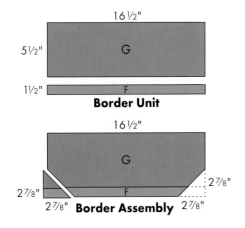

Border Unit

Border Assembly

5. Sew a C patch to each cut corner.

6. Make eighteen border units.

7. To make a corner unit, repeat Step 5 in one corner of an H patch.

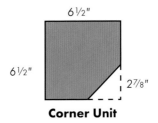

Corner Unit

8. Sew a C patch to the cut corner.

9. Make four corner units.

10. Join four border units end to end. Sew to the top of the quilt, matching the seams in the C patches. Refer to partial quilt assembly. Repeat for the bottom border.

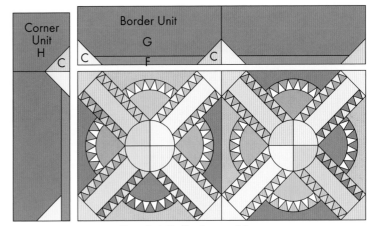

Partial Quilt Assembly

11. Join five border units end to end. Sew a corner unit to each end, turning the units as shown in the photo. Sew to the side of the quilt, matching the seams in the C patches. Repeat for the remaining side of the quilt.

12. Remove the paper.

Quilting and Finishing

1. Layer and baste the quilt backing, batting, and top.

2. Quilt in-the-ditch around the small triangles.

3. Trim quilt backing and batting even with the quilt top. Bind the quilt.

4. Join 2¼"-wide strips diagonally to make the binding.

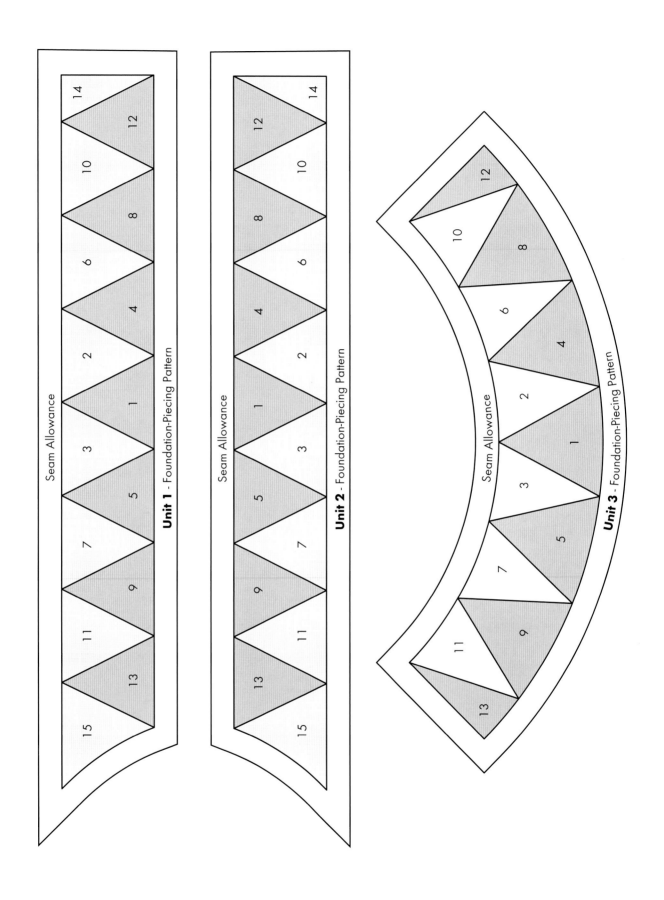

Seam Allowance

Unit 1 - Foundation-Piecing Pattern

Seam Allowance

Unit 2 - Foundation-Piecing Pattern

Seam Allowance

Unit 3 - Foundation-Piecing Pattern

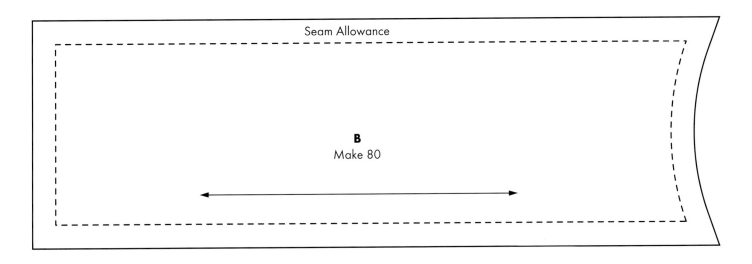

Seam Allowance

B
Make 80

Seam Allowance

C
Make 120

Match dots with seams
on adjacent patches.

Seam Allowance

D
Make 80

A
Make 80

*Align arrows with
lengthwise or crosswise
grain of fabric.*

Seam Allowance

½ E
Make 80

*Place
on fold
for E.*

Quilting Basics

General Guidelines

Seam Allowances

A $\frac{1}{4}$" seam allowance is used for most projects. It's a good idea to do a test seam before you begin sewing to check that your $\frac{1}{4}$" is accurate.

Pressing

In general, press seams toward the darker fabric. Press lightly in an up-and-down motion. Avoid using a very hot iron or over-ironing, which can distort shapes and blocks.

Borders

When border strips are to be cut on the crosswise grain, diagonally piece the strips together to achieve the needed lengths.

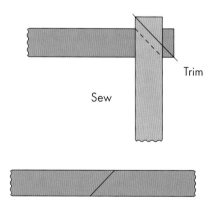

Sew

Trim

Butted Borders

In most cases the side borders are sewn on first. When you have finished the quilt top, measure it through the center vertically. This will be the length

to cut the side borders. Place pins at the centers of all four sides of the quilt top, as well as in the center of each side border strip. Pin the side borders to the quilt top first, matching the center pins. Using a $\frac{1}{4}$" seam allowance, sew the borders to the quilt top and press.

Measure horizontally across the center of the quilt top including the side borders. This will be the length to cut the top and bottom borders. Repeat pinning, sewing, and pressing.

Mitered Corner Borders

Measure the length of the quilt top and add two times the width of your border, plus 5". This is the length you need to cut or piece the side for borders.

Place pins at centers of both side borders and all four sides of the quilt top. From the center pin, measure in both directions, mark half of the measured length of the quilt top on both side borders. Pin, matching centers and the marked length of the side border to the edges of the quilt top. Stitch the strips to the sides of the quilt top. Stop and backstitch at the seam allowance line, $\frac{1}{4}$" in from the edge. The excess length will extend beyond each edge. Press seams toward border.

Start and stop stitching $\frac{1}{4}$" from edge.

Determine the length needed for the top and bottom border the same way, measuring the width of the quilt top through the center including each side border. Add 5" to this measurement. Cut or piece these border strips. From the center of each border strip, in both directions, mark half of the measured width of the quilt top. Again, pin, stitch up to the ¼" seamline, and backstitch. The border strips extend beyond each end.

To create the miter, lay the corner on the ironing board. Working with the quilt right side up, lay one strip on top of the adjacent border.

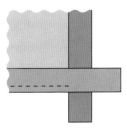

Fold the top border strip under itself so that it meets the edge of the outer border and forms a 45° angle. Press and pin the fold in place.

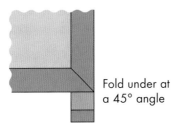

Fold under at a 45° angle

Position a 90° angle triangle or ruler over the corner to check that the corner is flat and square. When everything is in place press the fold firmly.

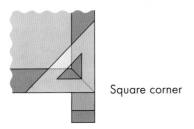

Square corner

Fold the center section of the top diagonally from the corner, right sides together, and align the long edges of the border strips. On the wrong side, place pins near the pressed fold in the corner to secure the border strips.

Beginning at the inside corner, backstitch and stitch along the fold toward the outside point, being careful not to allow any stretching to occur.

Backstitch at the end. Trim the excess border fabric to ¼" seam allowance. Press the seam open.

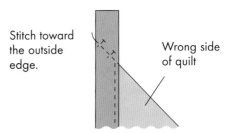

Stitch toward the outside edge.

Wrong side of quilt

Backing

Plan on making the backing a minimum of 2" larger than the quilt top on all sides. Prewash the fabric, and trim the selvages before you piece.

To economize, you can piece the back from any leftover fabrics or blocks in your collection.

Batting

The type of batting to use is a personal decision; consult your local quilt shop. Cut batting approximately 4" larger on all sides than your quilt top.

Layering

Spread the backing wrong side up and tape the edges down with masking tape. (If you are working on carpet you can use T-pins to secure the backing to the carpet.) Center the batting on top, smoothing out any folds. Place the quilt top right side up on top of the batting and backing, making sure it's centered.

Basting

If you plan to machine quilt, pin baste the quilt layers together with safety pins placed a minimum of 3"– 4" apart. Begin basting in the center and move toward the edges first in vertical, then horizontal, rows.

If you plan to hand quilt, baste the layers together with thread using a long needle and light-colored thread. Knot one end of the thread. Using stitches approximately the length of the needle, begin in the center and move out toward the edges.

Quilting

Quilting, whether by hand or machine, enhances the pieced or appliqué design of the quilt. You may choose to quilt in-the-ditch, echo the pieced or appliqué motifs, use patterns from quilting design books and stencils, or do your own free-motion quilting. Suggested quilting patterns are included in some of the projects.

Binding

Double Fold Straight Grain Binding (French Fold)

Trim excess batting and backing from the quilt. If you want a ¼" finished binding, cut the strips 2¼" wide and piece together with a diagonal seam to make a continuous binding strip.

Press the seams open, then press the entire strip in half lengthwise with wrong sides together. With raw edges even, pin the binding to the edge of the quilt a few inches away from the corner, and leave the first few inches of the binding unattached. Start sewing, using a ¼" seam allowance.

Stop ¼" away from the first corner (see Step 1), backstitch one stitch. Lift the presser foot and needle. Rotate the quilt one quarter turn. Fold the binding at a right angle so it extends straight above the quilt (see Step 2). Then bring the binding strip down even with the edge of the quilt (see Step 3). Begin sewing at the folded edge.

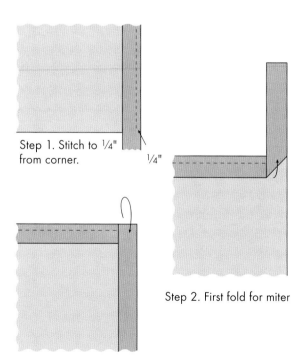

Step 1. Stitch to ¼" from corner.   ¼"

Step 2. First fold for miter

Step 3. Second fold alignment. Repeat in the same manner at all corners.

Continuous Bias Binding

A continuous bias involves using the same square sliced in half diagonally but sewing the triangles together so that you continuously cut the marked strips. The same instructions can be used to cut bias for piping. Cut the fabric for the bias binding or piping so it is a square. If yardage is ½ yard, cut an 18" square. Cut the square in half diagonally, creating two triangles.

Sew these triangles together as shown, using a ¼" seam allowance. Press the seam open.

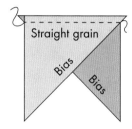

Straight grain

Bias   Bias

Using a ruler, mark the parallelogram with lines spaced the width you need to cut your bias. Cut along the first line about 5".

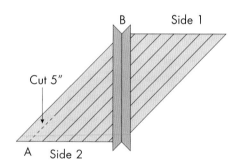

B   Side 1

Cut 5"

A   Side 2

Join Side 1 and Side 2 to form a tube. Line A will line up with the raw edge at B. This will allow the first line to be offset by one strip width. Pin the raw ends together, making sure that the lines match. Sew with a ¼" seam allowance. Press seams open.

Finishing the Binding

This is one method of finishing the binding. Fold under the beginning end of the binding strip ¼". Lay the ending binding strip over the beginning folded end. Continue stitching the seam beyond the folded edge. Trim the excess binding. Fold the binding over the raw edges to the quilt back and hand stitch, mitering corners.

Machine Appliqué Using Fusible Adhesive

Lay the fusible web sheet paper-side up on the pattern and trace with a pencil. Trace detail lines with a permanent marker for ease in transferring to the fabric.

Use paper-cutting scissors to roughly cut out the pieces. Leave at least a ¼" border.

Following manufacturer's instructions, fuse the web patterns to the wrong side of the appliqué fabric. It helps to use an appliqué-pressing sheet to avoid getting the adhesive on your iron or ironing board.

Cut out the pieces along the pencil line. Do not remove the paper yet.

Transfer the detail lines to the fabric by placing the piece on a light table or up to the window and marking the fabric. Use pencil for this task—the lines will be covered by thread.

Remove the paper and position the appliqué piece on your project. Be sure the web (rough) side is down. Press in place, following the manufacturer's instructions.

Paper Piecing

Once you get used to it, paper piecing is an easy way to ensure that your blocks will be accurate. You sew on the side of the paper with the printed lines. Fabric is placed on the non-printed side.

Trace or photocopy the number of paper-piecing patterns needed for your project.

Use a smaller-than-usual stitch length (#1.5–1.8 or 18 to 20 stitches per inch), and a slightly larger needle (size 90/14). This makes the paper removal easier and will result in tighter stitches that can't be pulled apart when you tear the paper off.

Cut the pieces slightly larger than necessary about ¾" larger; they do not need to be perfect shapes. (One of the joys of paper piecing!) With paper piecing you don't have to worry about the grain of the fabric. You are stitching on paper and that stabilizes the block. The paper is not torn off until after the blocks are stitched together.

Follow the number sequence when piecing. Pin piece #1 in place on the blank side of the paper, but make sure you don't place the pin anywhere near a seam line. Hold the paper up to the light to make sure the piece covers the area it is supposed to, with the seam allowance also amply covered. Fold the pattern back at the stitching line and trim the fabric to a ¼" seam allowance with a ruler and rotary cutter.

Cut piece #2 large enough to cover the area of #2 plus a generous seam allowance. It's a good idea to cut each piece larger than you think necessary; it might be a bit wasteful, but easier than ripping out tiny stitches! Align the edge with the trimmed seam allowance of piece #1, right sides together, and pin. Paper side up, stitch one line.

Open piece #2 and press.

Continue stitching each piece in order, being sure to fold back the paper pattern and trim the seam allowance to ¼" before adding the next piece.

Trim all around the finished unit to the ¼" seam allowance. Leave the paper intact until after the blocks have been sewn together, then carefully remove it. Creasing the paper at the seamline helps when tearing it.

Paper-Piecing Hints

- When making several identical blocks, it helps to work in assembly-line fashion. Add pieces #1 and #2 to each of the blocks, then add #3, and so on.
- Pre-cutting all the pieces at once is a time saver. Make one block first to ensure that each fabric piece will cover the area needed.
- When piecing a dark and a light fabric together where the seam allowance needs to be pressed toward the light fabric, the edge of the dark seam allowance will sometimes show through the light fabric. To prevent this, trim the dark seam allowance about $\frac{1}{16}$" narrower than the light seam allowance.

For more information write for a free catalog:
C&T publishing, Inc.
P.O. Box 1456
Lafayette, CA 94549
(800) 284-1114
e-mail: ctinfo@ctpub.com
website: www.ctpub.com

For quilting supplies:
Cotton Patch Mail Order
3405 Hall Lane, Dept. CTB
Lafayette, CA 94549
(800) 835-4418
(925) 283-7883
e-mail: quiltusa@yahoo.com
website: www.quiltusa.com
Note: Fabrics used in the quilts shown may not be currently available since fabric manufacturers keep most fabrics in print for only a short time.

Index